Praise for Stephani and Everyday Ki

"A lilting genius of the inner worlds."

—SARK, BEST-SELLING AUTHOR OF
SUCCULENT WILD WOMEN AND *EAT MANGOS NAKED*

"Through thoughtful observations and compelling stories, Dowrick models for the reader an effective way to consider the journey toward love of others and of self."

—*PUBLISHERS WEEKLY*

"[Dowrick's] wisdom is contagious. If anyone can cause a happiness revolution, she can."

—PAUL WILSON, INTERNATIONAL BEST-SELLING
AUTHOR OF *THE LITTLE BOOK OF CALM*

"Once again, Stephanie Dowrick has drawn on her extensive experience . . . to deliver a book that will appeal to anyone looking to improve the quality of their life. This is insightful, stimulating reading which will leave readers feeling positive about themselves."

—*BOOKSELLER & PUBLISHER* MAGAZINE (4-STAR REVIEW)

"Courageous and original, [Dowrick] asks the most difficult questions with enormous heart and intelligence."

—JOYCE REISER KORNBLATT, AUTHOR OF *THE REASON FOR WINGS*

"In *Everyday Kindness*, Stephanie Dowrick shows how a world of love and happiness is within our reach. Typical of Dowrick's work, *Everyday Kindness* is a warm, inspiring and engaging exploration of what it means to be happy and how the smallest acts of kindness can make all the difference. . . . [It is] highly personable and enlightening, making this a book that's especially relevant for our overworked and over-stressed culture."

—*WELLBEING* MAGAZINE

"Stephanie Dowrick is unashamed to make a stand for wonder and the incredible gift of living. Like so many thinkers before her, she recognizes that until we respect ourselves and begin to reflect this respect in our behavior toward others, we are diminished as individuals and as a society."

—WALTER MASON, AUTHOR OF *DESTINATION SAIGON*

"Dr. Stephanie Dowrick is making a calmer, happier and more rewarding life possible with this intimate, deeply reassuring book."

—*INSIGHT* MAGAZINE

"Stephanie Dowrick's words are like a soothing balm that she applies to our scratches and cuts and sometimes terrible pain. In *Everyday Kindness* she brings together the wisdom, experience and learning she has gained from a rich and varied life. . . . This is a perfect book to dip into."

—*THE SATURDAY AGE*

"This self-development book is helpful and wise. Stephanie Dowrick is renowned for her writing on relationships, spirituality, and how to foster a happy life. . . . This book is essentially a reflection on emotional intelligence and how to develop its gifts. Whether discussing parenting, friendship, love, housework, sex, diet, or alcohol, Dowrick provides the perceptive and practical advice you would welcome from a friend."

—*HERALD SUN*

Everyday Kindness

Also by Stephanie Dowrick

FICTION

Running Backwards Over Sand

Tasting Salt

NONFICTION

Intimacy and Solitude

The Intimacy & Solitude Self-Therapy Book

Forgiveness and Other Acts of Love

The Universal Heart

Free Thinking

Choosing Happiness

Creative Journal Writing

The Almost-Perfect Marriage

In the Company of Rilke

Seeking the Sacred

Everyday Kindness

*Shortcuts to a Happier and
More Confident Life*

STEPHANIE DOWRICK

JEREMY P. TARCHER/PENGUIN
a member of Penguin Group (USA) Inc.
New York

JEREMY P. TARCHER/PENGUIN
Published by the Penguin Group
Penguin Group (USA) Inc., 375 Hudson Street, New York, New York 10014, USA · Penguin Group
(Canada), 90 Eglinton Avenue East, Suite 700, Toronto, Ontario M4P 2Y3, Canada (a division of Pearson
Penguin Canada Inc.) · Penguin Books Ltd, 80 Strand, London WC2R 0RL, England · Penguin Ireland,
25 St Stephen's Green, Dublin 2, Ireland (a division of Penguin Books Ltd) · Penguin Group (Australia),
250 Camberwell Road, Camberwell, Victoria 3124, Australia (a division of Pearson Australia Group Pty Ltd) ·
Penguin Books India Pvt Ltd, 11 Community Centre, Panchsheel Park, New Delhi–110 017, India ·
Penguin Group (NZ), 67 Apollo Drive, Rosedale, North Shore 0632, New Zealand (a division
of Pearson New Zealand Ltd) · Penguin Books (South Africa) (Pty) Ltd,
24 Sturdee Avenue, Rosebank, Johannesburg 2196, South Africa

Penguin Books Ltd, Registered Offices: 80 Strand, London WC2R 0RL, England

Originally published in Australia as *Everyday Kindness* by Allen & Unwin in 2011.
First American edition published by Jeremy P. Tarcher in 2012.

Library of Congress Cataloging-in-Publication Data

Dowrick, Stephanie.
Everyday kindness : shortcuts to a happier and more confident life / Stephanie Dowrick. — 1st American ed.
p.   cm.
ISBN 978-0-399-16089-9
1. Kindness.   2. Conduct of life.   3. Happiness.   4. Self-esteem.   I. Title.
BJ1533.K5D69   2012   2012017644
177'.7—dc23

Printed in the United States of America
1   3   5   7   9   10   8   6   4   2

Book design by Meighan Cavanaugh

FOR MADELEINE

May the giving and receiving of kindness be your constant blessing.

"Three things in human life are important. The first is to be kind. The second is to be kind. The third is to be kind."

Henry James

"Be kind whenever possible. It is always possible."

His Holiness, the Dalai Lama

"The little unremembered acts of kindness and love are the best parts of a person's life."

William Wordsworth

"Kindness is twice blessed. It blesses the one who gives it . . . and the person who receives it."

Dawna Markova

CONTENTS

INTRODUCTION

✧

From the moment of our birth, we are dependent for our well-being on the kindness of others. What's more, to grow in confidence and self-trust, we are equally dependent on knowing that we can consistently and generously offer kindness *to* others.

Kindness is what gives life to our most tender, nourishing and consoling experiences. It soothes us and often makes us deeply happy. A kind thought or gesture, or a small act of consideration, is transformative. It can make us feel well. It can make the world seem good.

If we could pick up a telescope and look down the years of our lives, virtually every moment of our greatest happiness would reflect the giving and receiving of kindness. Just as crucially, we would see that the moments of our greatest suffering were made tolerable only through connection, comfort and kindness. In its many expressions (thoughtfulness, respect, interest, courtesy, compassion, concern), kindness is the quality that most obviously relies upon and expresses our emotional intelligence.

An attitude of kindness toward ourselves develops an appreciation for the greatest gift of all: our gift of life. Whether we are thinking about how to encourage ourselves, or about our relationship choices, or how we parent our children, get over disappointments, or support others in the community or workplace, we need to trust that we can do this compassionately and confidently.

If we are thinking about the food we eat and its effects on our bodies, our need to become physically or emotionally stronger, or to give up unhelpful habits and experiment with a more vibrant way of living, then we will do this far more effectively if we bypass helplessness and self-criticism and instead generate the enthusiasm and compassion that kindness allows. No less crucially, if we are considering the wider world and our capacity to influence events and opinions positively, then kindness, as an attitude and a value, will allow this.

Kindness will build our resilience and positivity, as well as concern for ourselves and others. It will protect us against the self-doubt or self-pity that would otherwise sap our strength. It will radically enhance our connections with others and our awareness of our capacity to give generously—and to reap the benefits that come with this. Bringing kindness into the bigger picture of our lives will wake up and utilize our powers to choose, and to choose wisely and well. It will make us less needy and much easier to like and to love.

OUR ACTS OF KINDNESS toward other people also depend on our consciousness of choice, and a willingness to take charge of our attitudes and actions. Those acts of kindness demonstrate a life-changing awareness that *other people matter*. This awareness is crucial. It's not just that a selfish life will be impoverished and causes misery. More than that, our safety as well as our happiness depends on the quality of our connections with other people—and on their connections with us. To flourish emotionally, we need other people. And they need us.

In one of the chapters of this book that I most enjoyed writing, I discuss pioneering psychologist William James's suggestion that "The deepest principle in human nature is the craving to be appreciated." *Kindness is the quality that brings appreciation—and consideration—to life.* In fact, I'm willing to say that we would live in a different world entirely if each of us truly refined our talents for kindness: if we took it as a privilege as well as a responsibility to create a kinder, safer, friendlier and far more appreciative world. It would also be a more peaceful world.

Such a world is within our reach.

SOME OF YOU will know that I have been writing about kindness for years. When I wrote about forgiveness, I was writing about kindness. When I wrote about happiness, I was writing about kindness. When I wrote about recovering and moving on, I was writing about kindness. When I wrote about parenting, intimacy, joy, making positive, uplifting choices around food or moods, I was writing about kindness. When I wrote about confidence, personal power, living more gratefully or creatively, or seeking God, I was writing about kindness. His Holiness the Dalai Lama has said that his religion is kindness. It is also a way of life, of being fully alive and engaged to the very last breath.

Neither passive nor always easy, the empathy and concern that drive kindness are fundamental in all of our connections, both with our own inner world and with others. In the absence of kindness, we suffer. In its presence, we flourish.

. . .

WHEN IT CAME to putting together this book of short chapters or articles, kindness came immediately to the foreground. *Everyday kindness* is such a simple phrase but it sings to me of hope. It describes what I believe is possible, each and every day of our lives. It embraces what I believe most of us yearn for: a spacious, trusting, harmonious and more confident life. This is a life where you can dare to think about yourself and your dilemmas supportively and effectively. It's a life where your needs count—but so do mine. It's a life where conflict happens. And can be dealt with. It's a life that includes your anxieties, setbacks, losses, grief and fears, but is not overwhelmed by them. It's a life that *notices what's going well*, and relishes that.

A life of everyday kindness welcomes challenge and stimulation, as well as peace. More than simply kind, it is sensual, appreciative, alert, resourceful and engaged.

THERE IS NO ASPECT of daily living where kindness fails to make a difference. It softens the heart, yet, in terms of the resolve and clarity it needs, it also makes us stronger.

Remembering how integral kindness is to our well-being, these short chapters—each written for you to read at a single sitting—cover a variety of topics that themselves reflect the scope of most of our lives.

The everyday *is* our conversation here. That includes thinking freshly about what we eat as well as think; how influenced we are or need to be by upbringing, gender, moods or opinions; where and when our instincts could rescue us; having more power—and sharing it; what soothes us most effectively, as well as our children; what we are newly discovering about the brain as well as the emotions; what makes us more joyful and alive; what relieves our suffering and heals our hearts. It includes a range of significant work dilemmas as well as many parenting ones. It lets us face with greater confidence being young and growing older. And it offers a way out of some common difficulties in intimate and family relationships where our need for kindness is often greatest.

A NUMBER of these chapters first took shape in the "Inner Life" column I wrote with such pleasure for nine years for *Good Weekend* (the weekend supplement to the *Sydney Morning Herald* and Melbourne's *The Age*). As intensely as I wrote and rewrote them at the time, however, none has survived intact. Moving them from the magazine to the pages of this book, I rethought and expanded them, inspired not just by my own new thinking but also by this powerful and empowering theme of kindness. Other chapters began on my website or Facebook pages, where I continue to write and meet (and interact with) new readers. More chapters than I had expected were written expressly for this book.

Writing has been my principal work for more than twenty-five years, and alongside the books (which often need years to complete), I have always written shorter articles and reviews. But it was those years of writing for *Good Weekend* that convinced me how pleasurable it can be to write focused, short chapters like these. I discovered how stimulating the intensity is of pursuing a single theme. And I know from your comments that while many of you (like me) love to lose yourself in a longer book, you also like the particular pleasure of reading a self-contained chapter or article and thinking about that before moving on.

. . .

THERE'S A SENSE of reunion here that has been deeply sustaining and sometimes exhilarating. *Everyday Kindness* has given me reason to return to the values that matter most to me, and perhaps also to you. Kindness and encouragement run through my work like a theme tune: continuing reminders of what will make a difference; continuing confidence that this is a difference each of us can and must make. But there is always more to know and, creating this book, some of that has emerged for me on and off the page.

FOR YEARS NOW I have been giving well-being talks on a regular basis for Breast Cancer Network Australia, an organization that itself demonstrates kindness, thoughtfulness and enterprise in all that it does. At the end of my presentations I include a slide that says, "May the blessings of peace and kindness be with you always."

These are blessings we all need, whether or not our lives have been touched by serious illness. They are blessings we need. They are blessings we can give. And they are exquisite in their ordinariness.

The so-called ordinariness of everyday living has grown increasingly precious to me. It's where our happiness is lost—or found. It's where kindness is discovered and refined. Kindness can be the language and mode of that daily existence. Knowing that, I wish you the joy of a kinder life, not today only, but always.

Making a Difference

❋

Whether you are conscious of it or not, it's in your power to increase other people's joy, satisfaction and safety through simple acts of kindness. A thoughtful word, a smile or acknowledgment, giving something that's needed, listening with care, extending your patience, expressing your concern appreciatively, ordinary courtesies, refraining from criticism or outbursts, acknowledging someone else's point of view or legitimate needs, making time for someone who is struggling, assuming the best: that power is worth everything. It's the basis of your confidence in yourself. It lets you know that regardless of what is happening outside your control, *your life is vital, sustaining and absolutely worth living*.

KINDNESS drives connection and engagement, empathy and comfort. It is thoughtfulness in action. It is self-respect and concern for others in action.

Kindness lets you live life to the full. It expresses your gratitude for *who you are and what you can contribute*.

You can't become kinder to others without also benefiting

yourself. You can't be more genuinely self-supportive without also asking and needing less of others—and benefiting them also.

KINDNESS doesn't mean surrendering your boundaries or meeting every demand that comes your way. It doesn't mean becoming a doormat that others can walk over. It can mean being much clearer about saying no as well as yes. Nonetheless, kindness pushes you to take other people into account constantly, even while it also saves you from harming, demeaning or sacrificing yourself.

Kindness helps you physically as much as it does emotionally and spiritually. It keeps you connected. It relaxes you. It radically reduces tension and stress. It doesn't depend upon status, education or wealth. It doesn't depend upon brilliance or age. And it certainly can't depend only on things always going well for you. (Easy to be kind when everything is going our way. Far more vital to be kind when life is *not* going our way.)

KINDNESS, as a way of life and living, depends on choices made and remade on a daily basis. Sometimes it will be self-evident and easy. Sometimes it will be an effort. Sometimes it will seem intuitive. Sometimes we will have to silence those self-righteous reasons why we should *not* be kind.

Perhaps we learn most about kindness when we have to think about it, when we are forced by circumstances to leave our comfort zone, question our emotional habits and think hard about the effect of what we are doing or saying. It is particularly powerful when we can be kind for kindness's sake and because we are free to be kind, rather than because it will make us a hero in other people's eyes or win us favors.

Many regard kindness as something sweet. It *can* sweeten life, sometimes immeasurably. But in practice and as an ideal, it is far tougher than sweet. Whoever we are, and however much self-awareness we have, to behave and live with kindness challenges our egocentricity and the delusion that we are the center of the universe with needs that should always take precedence over others.

KINDNESS is learned moment by moment. But it will always carry most weight when we take it up as a fundamental attitude rather than as a series of individual acts: when we see it as cause *and* as effect.

New Day, New Chance

※

One of my favorite ways to keep my life in balance is to notice something new each day that I can consciously appreciate. Ideally, it's something that I haven't noticed before. And on my way to making my choice of the day, I will invariably review and appreciate other moments also.

This small inner discipline is a challenge both to my creativity and powers of observation. It keeps me awake. It keeps me in the moment rather than constantly stirring the past or looking to an unknown future.

Kindness can be a similar catalyst. Finding fresh ways each day to express our thoughtfulness or kindness deepens our engagement with other people. It makes other people's lives more real to us. It throws us more deeply into life. It certainly saves us from helplessness and self-pity. It brings beauty and it is beauty.

As an idea, kindness is already a small miracle. For this small miracle to live, we must embody it and give it life. We must think harder about what will lift other people's spirits. (Often it's the same acts of appreciation and thoughtfulness that will lift our own spirits.)

We must refuse those ubiquitous temptations to snap (because we are tired), argue (because we are irritable), criticize (because we are out of sorts) or gossip (because we are bored).

There can surely be no finer words of appreciation than "How kind that person is!" *That person* can be you.

All About You

❊

There is only one relationship that runs through each moment of your life: the one you have with your own self. It will shape every other relationship and encounter you will have, yet even (and perhaps especially) in this age of rampant self-focus many people find this relationship with self as confusing as any other.

In fact, I suspect that vast numbers of people will do almost anything to avoid even the most superficial processes of reflection. This leaves them stranded when it comes to knowing what their values or inner strengths are. They may also struggle to take responsibility for the life they are creating—particularly when things are not going well. They may tell you very frankly that they hate to spend too much time in their own company. They may remain blithely ignorant of how they affect other people and what it means to put their own agenda aside when it clashes with someone else's.

THE IDEA of taking your inner world in the least bit seriously is easily mocked. Relentless superficiality shrieks for our attention. Doing things that take time, concentration and personal effort is increasingly out of favor. Yet one of the harshest features of contemporary life is that we are often pushed to meet an increasingly complex world without the skills of self-awareness and reflection. And with increasingly less of the time and patience that we need to refuel ourselves at the deepest levels.

I heard a prominent businessman speak recently of his years of untreated depression in the midst of outstanding success, and his profound regret that in his race to the illusory "top" he had allowed himself no time to "smell the roses." This almost cost him his life, because his depression was treated only after a very public suicide attempt.

His was a brave admission. What it meant to me was that he had too little time to be present to the precious moments of *being*, of appreciating life and recovering a sense of himself before hurtling into the next demand. Those incessant demands in his life, or in yours or mine, may well be exciting and challenging. In excess, though, they can tip us dangerously out of balance.

THESE ARE NOT new themes. One of the great joys in my writing life has been my work on the visionary poet Rainer Maria Rilke. Almost a hundred years ago he warned against the psychic and emotional losses or even devastation that come when we constantly override our deepest needs, or find no language to give them meaning.

Treating ourselves like machines doesn't turn us into machines. If we are at work almost all our waking hours, then rushing in the few hours left to meet a whole variety of practical household demands, or "partying hard" before returning to work again, any downtime is likely to feel dangerously flat rather than restorative. The contrast can seem too stark for the adrenaline addicted. And that sets up a dangerous pattern. Fearing emptiness or boredom even more than exhaustion, something crucial is lost: the stable, trusting relationship with yourself, which will be, in turn, the well from which you draw in all your other relationships.

IN THE BUSIEST of lives, stillness and focus are needed. Without that, we will feel severely out of balance. Sometimes this is reflected in erratic moods. Sometimes—perhaps often—it leads to illness.

Stillness doesn't mean lying on the sofa in front of a television set (though a little passive entertainment like that goes a long way). It means allowing your mind to settle or rest on something that also lifts your spirits: something that engages you even while it soothes you.

Many people listen to beautiful music, allowing their thoughts to drift as they do so, or take time (and take *their* time) in nature. Or they read something brief like a poem or prayer that allows them the space also to muse and let the mind wander. Or they write in their journal, emptying out their thoughts onto the page and feeling a surprising degree of peace when they have done so. Many walk with no sense of purpose other than the walk itself. Some will simply sit, watching their thoughts arise and fall, rather as they might watch clouds moving across a deep blue sky.

They might call this time meditation. Or even child care.

A young father told me recently, "I love the quiet time in the night when my wife is sleeping and I am the one holding our baby. There's just us, tiny Isaac asleep on my chest and me sitting in the dark, getting to know one another with quiet all around. I know how brief this time will be and I am still amazed how much I am enjoying it."

. . .

OUR EASE OF MIND depends upon our capacity to relax into our own company and be refreshed by it, rather than avoiding it. Years ago Irish novelist Edna O'Brien wrote, "All my life I feared the places where one faced the self without distraction, without the crutches of other people."

That fear is widespread—and often intensified by legitimate concerns about selfishness and self-absorption. Yet we also know that the endless self-focused talk that pours out of many people doesn't signal inner confidence or self-acceptance. And that hectically avoiding your own company doesn't necessarily add up to your being terrific company for others.

HOW WE FEEL about ourselves is demonstrated on a daily basis by what we avoid as well as what we embrace. Self-respect needs to be part of that story. So does self-trust. Both those qualities have their best chance to emerge not through outer achievement only but also through *having time for ourselves*, time to discover ourselves, not least through knowing what will soothe, inspire or revive us.

Kind to Yourself

The person many of us find most difficult to be kind to is our own self. Yet until we know how to be kind to ourselves, our kindness to others will always be hedged and conditional. And our self-confidence will always be fragile.

There is a lovely midpoint between debilitating self-criticism and self-doubt (or self-loathing) and treating yourself like the only person in the universe whose life counts. Yet it's often surprisingly difficult to find that midpoint and stick to it.

I used to think that mine was going to be the last generation brought up with the horrible idea that you must behave like a punitive ogre toward yourself if you are not to become spoiled, lazy and self-indulgent. But I was quite wrong. Not just my own but also subsequent generations seem as skilled as ever at putting themselves down, talking about themselves in blistering terms or maintaining an inner commentary of self-talk that's ugly at best and despairing at worst. Many also take tragic risks with their lives. Or grossly underestimate their capacity to do without the props of alcohol or drugs.

Defensive, self-protective behaviors can be just as corrosive and can keep someone just as inwardly unsettled. These might include rudeness in all its guises, talking about yourself incessantly, boasting, controlling, finding compromise impossible, making a huge fuss when things don't go your way, and taking little real interest in other people and their needs or stories.

PSYCHOLOGICAL RESEARCH long ago proved that children must feel positive about themselves if they are to flourish and grow caring of others. They need to know how to be kind to themselves. And they need to know what kindness means.

To learn this, children need positive messages and examples from adults—most of all from their parents. They need enthusiasm, trust and a keen focus on what's going right rather than endlessly dwelling on what's gone wrong or what might go wrong.

Adults need that kind of nurturing also. They need to be able to soothe themselves when they are agitated, encourage themselves when facing something difficult, get over small mistakes and learn fast from bigger ones. They need to grow strong inwardly as well as outwardly, value their resilience and robustness, and be quite clear about what supports those qualities.

As long as they believe they are doomed to their poor opinion of themselves, they are likely to spend countless hours trying to second-guess what other people think of them and drawing some sense of inner security from that. They may feel desperate for praise and kindness. Yet when praise and kindness come their way, they may find these gifts hard to take seriously.

This isn't surprising. When we don't trust ourselves, we easily mistrust how other people feel about us. We also mistrust other people's kindness and especially their efforts to reassure us: "She doesn't mean it. She's only saying that to make me feel better. . . ."

THE GOOD NEWS is that *you learn a kinder way of life by living it.* Theories are not enough. Good intentions are only the beginning.

It is liberating, sometimes even exhilarating, to discover that you can *choose* to talk to yourself far more positively, kindly and enthusiastically. And to discover how this is strengthening, not weakening, your sense of self. Sometimes people are quite unaware how dreary or negative their thoughts or behaviors are until something goes badly wrong. Or something pushes them to a new level of awareness.

Observing how you think, and particularly the effects of this on your body and emotions, is one way to get clarity. So is noticing the effect of your attitudes and choices on the people around you. Behaving more kindly toward yourself, your needs and resentments diminish. You let others off the hook.

Living more kindly, you can afford to be grateful for other people's ordinarily human, imperfect efforts. You don't have to require them to compensate for your lack of inner security, your emptiness or, at worst, your self-hatred. You don't need to nitpick, envy or spoil others' pleasure. You don't need to control. You become easier to be around. You become easier to like, understand and love.

The Kindness Effect

❀

In a period of less than two years, I twice went on retreat to India. My destination was Mount Abu, spiritual home of the Brahma Kumaris. As someone who leads retreats as well as attends them, I am aware that taking time out like that is a privilege. Getting up in the chilly dark for 4 a.m. meditation was, in those lovely circumstances, easy and a joy. But the privilege that struck me most forcibly was spending a week with people who were, to a person, unfailingly kind.

Of course it is easy to be kind when relatively little is being asked of you and a great deal is being done for you. But this was true only for the people like me who were actually on retreat. Many of those making life delightful for us were working hard. Their day also began with predawn meditation and it didn't end until fifteen or sixteen hours later. Yet their kindness never wavered.

BEING ON RETREAT is one of the purest experiences imaginable. To have kindness as our daily currency is deeply healing as well as heartening. But this is not the world most of us live in. And it may not be the world we easily know how to create.

As I was coming home, it was impossible to avoid a degree of shock at how many "normal" interactions between people are anything but kind. People hurt one another recklessly. They spit out their aggression and frustrations. They put others down. They demonstrate their irritation or contempt. They push and shove. They ignore the small courtesies. They shout. They whine. They demand. They ignore or countermand what's important to others if it isn't important to them. And if they stop to think about this at all, I suspect that they tell themselves it doesn't matter.

OUR OWN eager delight in the kindness of others, and gratitude for it, should tell us clearly that kindness matters. And that in every situation there are chances to be a little kinder, if only we would take them.

We know that. Even without the inspiration of a spiritual retreat, we know that. So why aren't we kinder routinely? Why don't we relish kindness? Why don't we praise it, sing it to the skies? Why don't we encourage thoughtfulness, even selflessness in our children and each other through example, praise, unqualified appreciation and delight?

Why don't we make kindness *our business*?

Behaving kindly, we demonstrate self-mastery *and* care for others. We demonstrate our willingness to care *and* to be caring. This brings us into harmony with other people. It lets us feel "of a piece" inside ourselves. We are choosing. And we are choosing wisely.

AND WHEN this goes wrong?

People may fail to be kind because they can't see how their

behavior affects other people. Or they don't care enough to want to make a difference. They may also be so self-absorbed that they can't take seriously anyone's feelings other than their own. They may tell themselves that the world has been horrible to them and that their actions are justified. They may be lazy. Or careless. When things get nasty, they may take pleasure in their own negativity. Or believe (wrongly) that withholding kindness or being unkind not only gains them attention but also gives them power.

They may also be projecting their own inner feelings of worthlessness onto other people, shoring up a weak ego by making other people wrong, bad or stupid. (We see lots of that in the political and business worlds and, sadly, in the least happy families.)

Those impulses away from kindness are familiar. But if we are to make the least claim to psychological maturity, and the least contribution to a happier, kinder, more generous world, then we have to transcend them.

We are, after all, interdependent as well as dependent. To get along well in this world, we have no choice but to take other people's well-being as seriously as our own. We need to claim the power we have to lift the spirits of other people. And lift our own spirits along with them.

Turning Points

I t is fascinating to consider why some people learn the languages of kindness and consideration while others plainly don't. Conventional intelligence is not a factor here. Some quite brilliant people are devoid of empathy and brutally unkind. They may even use their brilliance to be less kind, not realizing how impoverished this declares them to be.

THE PSYCHOLOGICAL rule of thumb used to be that a capacity for kindness—and the self-awareness as well as empathy that drives it—is established in infancy. And that it is dependent on the quality of the parents' interactions with their baby.

Loving constancy, or constant kindness, *is* the best start we can give to an infant or child. As a parental goal it remains unchallenged. But don't we all know people who were deeply loved, yet grew up to be selfish, shallow and sometimes nasty? And don't we also know real saints whose earliest years were bleak?

Some fortunate individuals have what seems like a genuine talent for kindness. But the story doesn't end there.

It's obvious we should give children their best possible chance by loving them unconditionally. And by teaching them kindness and concern through the way that we ourselves live. They need to see and experience how respect and kindness go hand in hand. And that living kindly takes tenacity and strength—and also builds these qualities. We need to see children as capable of learning these most basic lessons. And not just learning them, *living them*.

All of this takes considerable fortitude. But it will let children understand the power they have to *offer* kindness (thoughtfulness, courtesy, consideration) as well as receive it. And at least to glimpse how thinking more inclusively builds character and vital inner confidence in ways that aggressive self-interest or plain indifference never could.

BEYOND CHILDHOOD, other quite splendid saving factors also play a part.

We can learn something vital from our own hurts: from what others didn't do; from what others did in ways that diminished our happiness. We can discover what it means to be resolute about the kind of person we want to be and who we want others to know, see and experience.

We can learn something from the absence of courtesy—and how graceless this is. (It's as unattractive in children as it is in adults.)

We can discover and rediscover our power to choose, knowing that on the most ordinary day, whatever our psychological history, there are countless turning points when we can make it our business to behave more kindly and thoughtfully—or not. There are moments when we can begin to say something mean or remain silent; when we can withhold something generous or give it; when we can give way to a "bad mood" or get over it; when we can destroy someone's happiness or enhance it; when we can see the world through someone else's eyes, or choose to remain locked into our own limited point of view.

Those everyday choices—and especially our power to exercise them—may have as much influence on our current life and well-being as our parents ever did. Just as inevitably, they will determine the kind of wider society we want, and are collectively creating.

Grieving and Consoling

※

G rief is hard for most of us to think or talk about. And it's excruciating to bear. That makes it difficult for many of us to know how to give comfort to others when they are grieving. It may also make it difficult to receive comfort, even when it's sorely needed.

I have been thinking about grief a good deal over the past weeks as I have been reading a quite remarkable memoir from gifted writer Virginia Lloyd. It's called *The Young Widow's Book of Home Improvement* and it describes Virginia's passionate relationship with her husband, John, whom she met when she was thirty-two. He adored her. She adored him. At thirty-three, she married him. At thirty-four, Virginia was a widow.

Somehow I missed the book when it was first published but, reading it a little later, I was transfixed by the skill and subtlety Virginia uses to capture the complex and sometimes wildly varying emotions that we lump together and call grief. There is nothing predictable about this state of mind and heart. Even from one day to the next, but especially in the earliest weeks and months, devastating grief can display itself in many different ways.

I wept when I read Virginia's words:

At unexpected moments I found myself overpowered by a wave of grief that swamped without warning. When I reached for a saucepan in its cluttered drawer; when I folded the sheets, washed and dried, to put them away; when I sat on the couch flicking through a magazine; sometimes while I stood in the hallway, keys still in my hand from letting myself in the front door. On occasion these waves of grief literally felled me: I dropped to the ground, slumped as if the puppet strings I had been relying on to hold me up had failed.

THE PHYSICALITY of grief is shocking for many people. I've heard people say that it is as though their vital organs are wailing. And I understand that. Your body might hurt as much as your emotional heart. Food tastes like chalk. Your sleep is chaotic and so are your dreams and thoughts. It is difficult to concentrate and you may feel simultaneously highly sensitive to other people and weirdly indifferent.

It's also true that each of us will have our own patterns of reaction. Sometimes these will be literally incomprehensible to others. If it is our role to be the consoler, then we need to be extremely cautious about how we judge the intensity of someone else's reactions and emotions, particularly if they seem to be coping by losing themselves in a mad round of activity, as though they now have to live more wholeheartedly and not less.

Virginia's book also pushed me to reflect on whether the pain of grief is worse when the death is untimely or premature: when someone feels cheated of years they might fairly have expected with their loved one, and is aware of all that their loved one, too, is missing. Outrage as well as rage is often part of grieving. And when someone's life is cut short, there is likely to be a piercing sense of injustice as well as loss that will always make grieving extremely hard. Yet, when it comes to grief, I think we have to be cautious about what we call "worse."

The loss of a loved one is always hard. The grieving we do will almost always be intense and somewhat unpredictable, most of all in the early months or even years. At any stage, there is no "right" way to grieve, nor any one right way to console. Treating yourself compassionately and gently, and especially accepting the unpredictability of grief's demands, helps a little. So does accepting the consolation and concern of others, even when their efforts are far from perfect.

Your Best Coach, 24/7

A recent conversation reminded me how routinely so many people put themselves down, or make their lives more fear bound than perhaps they need to be.

I was at a conference, talking for some time during a long break with a thoughtful young woman in her late twenties. We had moved away from the topic of the day and she was telling me a little about her life and ideals when quite suddenly she made a harsh comment about herself, speaking callously about her looks. Then, as we were saying good-bye, she did something similar, although this time she was talking about her work goals. "I work with so many talented people," she said, "and often wonder where I fit in."

This time I questioned her. Was she appreciated at work? Had she been promoted? Was she receiving positive feedback from her clients? She answered yes to all my questions. I went on to ask about the basis of her pessimism. She looked vague and then said that she knew herself better than her colleagues or clients did.

What she didn't say, but I could surmise, was that she felt as though her success was somehow fraudulent and that one day people would see the anxious, insecure woman on the inside, rather than the polished, confident woman she appears to be.

THIS IS A SCENARIO I understand all too well. My own book, *Intimacy and Solitude*, was certainly precipitated by the fact that as a successful, confident young London publisher I continued to suffer anxiety about my deeper and far more vital sense of reality and self-worth.

Feeling different on the inside from the person others see on the outside is exhausting. I found it particularly painful when I would give a speech or go to a significant meeting where some degree of public performance was required. I knew that others saw me as confident and on top of things, even eloquent, but I would often go home feeling scooped out and empty. I would obsess about any real or imagined "mistakes" and rarely take in or enjoy the efforts that I had made, much less any real sense of achievement or gratification for them.

YEARS OF WRITING, psychotherapy and especially being a parent, as well as getting older, have helped me immeasurably. My spiritual life (and practices) has also made a huge difference, and I write about this and the secure sense of identity this has given me in the memoir sections of *Seeking the Sacred*. But those memories of my younger self are still vivid. I certainly know that without a secure sense of your own value, your self-criticism and fear of other people's judgments (and especially your fantasies about those judgments) will loom far too large.

This makes it hard to bounce back when things go wrong—as they sometimes will. Just as worryingly, you may well live with debilitating levels of anxiety or depression. Other people's support, praise and kindness may feel relatively meaningless.

Those inner struggles will inevitably affect your personal connections as well as your friendships and work life. The more intimate the relationship, the more we long to be loved for ourselves. But if you are unsure who that self is, or have fallen into bad habits of routinely putting yourself down, then it may feel confronting or inauthentic, rather than welcome, when the love you long for does come your way.

MANY PEOPLE struggling hardest or most constantly with issues of self-acceptance or self-esteem are, like the young woman from the conference, quite clearly sensitive and responsible. They may also be perfectionists.

In fact, they may often set themselves exhaustingly high standards while simultaneously berating themselves for ordinary human errors. Doing this, they remain dangerously vulnerable to even mild or perceived criticism, because this so neatly dovetails with their own fears. Constant anxiety about their life's value and authenticity is exhausting. And yet the outlook certainly is not grim.

My observation is that such people are often noticeably thoughtful toward others. This means that with support, *they can learn to direct some of that kindness toward themselves.*

Many people are unaware of how much of their conversation is about what didn't go well . . . how exhausted they are . . . how hopeless . . . how pathetic. It may even relate to their looks: how ugly they are . . . how fat . . . how unappealing.

Such thinking is virtually hypnotic. But it can be changed. *We can change it*. We can switch to another channel of thinking. We can refuse to engage with or pander to those negative inner remarks ("Oh, not that boring litany yet again . . ."). We can discover, in our own way, how to create an effective sense of distance from other people's actual or assumed criticisms by being far less entranced by the unfair, unhelpful things we say to ourselves.

SOMEONE CAUGHT UP in the snarls of their own negativity will also need to face their fears of making mistakes—or of being seen to make a mistake. When the fear of being wrong rules our thinking, it is often not just a matter of fearing doing something wrong but of feeling "all wrong" inside ourselves. That's what can make mistakes, criticism or other people's indifference seem so catastrophic. When we see more clearly what's going on, we are far less likely to be thrown by something relatively minor. And in the face of something more confronting, we can find out what's needed, rather than collapsing or fleeing.

WITH INSIGHT and acceptance, we can have a more relaxed sense of self. Valuing our own lives more—not for what we can do with them, but for the gift they intrinsically are—already makes a significant difference. We can also teach ourselves to focus on and enjoy what is going right, writing that down in a journal while we are learning new habits of thinking, then talking about it and doing more of it. (Writing something down in a journal is quite different and far more effective than just turning it over in your thoughts.)

We can successfully guide and coach ourselves through life's harder moments, discovering and calling on the strengths we need. We can appreciate more openly what other people are doing for us. We can take time and space to appreciate our own small triumphs or quiet successes.

EACH OF US spends every hour of every day in our own company. We need to make sure that company is *good*. Discovering that we can have our own best interests at heart, we will relish the moments we share with others. And we will become much more trusting of our own solid authenticity.

Beauty That Endures

Look in the mirror and chances are that the person looking back at you bears only a passing resemblance to who you are. There are certainly some people who gaze in the mirror and see someone loved, appreciated and familiar. But the rest?

They look in the mirror and first see what's wrong. Or what they tell themselves is wrong. That spot? Bright red, like a beacon. That nose? Longer than Pinocchio's. Those lines? Like ancient carvings. Those gray-green eyes so many people have gazed deeply into and admired? Overlooked entirely.

A few years ago when I was working on *Choosing Happiness*, I had a wonderful time writing the headings for that book's many short sections. One that I like best is "You are bigger than your dress size."

When I mention this in public it always makes people laugh. And then squirm. Because the truth is most women long to be much smaller than their dress size, whatever that size may be. Or if someone is a "perfect" size—whatever that means—then it's their hair that's wrong, or their age, or their mouth, ears, bottom, stomach. . . . Variations on the theme of dissatisfaction are literally endless. And the sad truth is that even if most women do manage to change their dress size, their concerns will find a new target and the cycle of anxiety and self-doubt will continue.

THIS EPIDEMIC of dissatisfaction is affecting girls as young as six. It's also troubling older women who should know better. Men are not exempt either. They often long to be taller or more muscular or to have more hair on their head rather than growing out of their ears or down their back. But the situation is undeniably worse for women. If anyone dares suggest we live in a postfeminist world, they should consider how superficially and cruelly women are discussed in relation to their physical appearance. And how unkindly some women talk about one another, or themselves.

The crazy thing is that this exhausting pursuit of beauty is rarely driven by considerations of happiness or well-being. It's not even much about beauty. It's basically about reassurance and a wholly externalized sense of being "all right." But feeling and knowing that you are all right won't happen with a change of size or style.

IT'S NOT NEWS that people who are young, thin and beautiful are no happier than the rest of us. Many of the world's most beautiful are apparently not happy at all. Exceptional beauty may itself be a cause for anxiety. "Do people only like me for my looks? Who will I be when my looks are gone? How can I hang on to this magic for the longest possible time?"

This is not to say appearance doesn't matter. It does. Getting physically fit and staying in good shape is terrific for health and well-being. Dressing smartly or with flair is a genuine pleasure. (I talk about clothes with my publisher, Sue, on a regular basis, along

with books, world affairs, the world of publishing, our children. . . .)
But "dressing for success" while starving or obsessing about your
looks never lifted anyone's spirits. In fact, it depresses them. And
focusing on physical appearance as key to your place in the world is
a colossal distraction from the main game.

WHAT'S MOST attractive in both women and men is a palpable
sense of being engaged with life, of being interested, generous,
appreciative and as alive as it is possible to be. It is also great to feel
positive about yourself. But this can't be about your looks only.

Well-being has to arise from a far more fundamental sense of
who you are. Someone who enjoys life and loves people will always
be a beauty in the eyes of others, whatever their actual age, shape or
size. What's more, such people will always find life beautiful, even
in its shadows and complexity.

Attitude is the key ingredient here. When you feel anxious or
unhappy, all the face peels or lifts in the world won't make a significant difference. When you feel good inside and good about life and
living, the "face" with which you face the world will reflect that.

IN ALL ITS GUISES, kindness sits lightly on our physical being,
whatever our size or age. Kindness may, in fact, be the greatest
beauty treatment of all, transforming us in the eyes of others and
making it possible for us to look into a mirror with good humor,
gratitude and grace.

Much Ado About Everything

୫

So much of the noisy agitation that whirls around us on a constant basis seems truly unnecessary. Yet we are so used to it, we may be tempted to think it is inevitable. Just days ago I was in a crowded city café and, along with everyone else present, was a reluctant witness to a well-dressed man throwing a temper tantrum that would have put the loudest terrible-two-year-old in the shade. Had his coffee arrived too hot or too cold? Was it skim, not soy? What about his sandwich? Had that failed to appear?

Whatever the problem, his outrage was . . . outrageous. I drank my own coffee as fast as I could and ran, aware as I went that people employed in all kinds of service industries are exposed to such tempests on a regular basis. More serious still is the situation for the people who are working or (worse) living with someone with so little tolerance for the small inconveniences of life.

But what also struck me with a great deal of force was how uncomfortable and destructive of peace of mind and happiness it is to *be* such a person, living in the eye of a storm.

. . .

IN THE COURSE of a day, all kinds of things can and will go adrift in our lives. Meeting those moments, what will matter most is not so much what that outer event is but *what it provokes in us.*

When we feel so strung out, anxious, frustrated or irritable that a relatively minor matter pushes us over the edge, this is a clear warning sign that all is not well with our inner world. We might well believe—and tell ourselves—that there are convincing reasons why our frustration buttons have been pushed. There may always be someone or something else we can blame. Yet even the most volatile among us will surely recognize that some days are better than others and that our reactions are often highly *dis*proportionate to whatever has enflamed us.

IT'S A NECESSARY SHOCK of childhood to discover that the world will not always bow to our agenda. *Things will go wrong.* Some of them will be other people's "fault"; some we will cause; some will be random. None of us would ever confess to believing that things ought to go our way all of the time. But our reaction when things do go awry may tell a different story.

If you routinely fuss about trivial matters you will be exhausting to be around. You may also be frightening. You will certainly be far less likable than you could be. None of that supports your closest relationships or sense of self. Yet in almost every situation you have at least some choice, perhaps not about what has happened but about how you will respond.

When it comes to everyday setbacks, you can resolve and choose to fuss much less.

Taking even a moment to reflect, you can see how your view is determined by your moods, physical health, tiredness or hunger— or whether this is the first or fortieth setback of the day. You can take those responses and yourself in hand. You can deal with the biggest issues in your life so that every trivial matter does not feel like the last straw. You can check if you are depressed or anxious and get effective help.

It's when we feel out of control emotionally that we most want to control everything around us. And we can't. What we do need to control is our own self.

THIS IS HARDER for some people to learn than for others. A rigid personality; self-pity or helplessness; untreated anxiety or depression; stress that's made worse by exhaustion, hunger or alcohol; habits of thinking that find fault: these are all factors that can get in the way. But none is terminal.

A far more agreeable way of living also depends on attitude and choice. Have fun experimenting with how good it feels to be a little more good-humored. *Grow your patience.* Assume that your agenda cannot and will not always prevail. Make it a daily practice to notice and talk about what's right, rather than what's wrong. Carry an internal measuring stick so you can instantly tell the truly important from all the rest.

Easier relationships, far less tension and significantly more personal power are within virtually everyone's reach. Not a bad trade-off for silencing a fuss.

Worrying Well

Many psychotherapists in private practice, as I once was, largely work with the "worried well." These people are not mentally ill and are generally not in need of medication or hospitalization. Nonetheless, they recognize that they are living with less joy and perhaps more anxiety, worry and self-doubt than is desirable. And, wonderfully, they are prepared to do something about it.

Worry is very much part of the contemporary emotional landscape. So it was with real interest that I found myself involved in a recent lively conversation about the value of worry, whether worry is inevitable and if it's ever productive. One man in his late thirties described sitting in a hospital at the bedside of his only child, consciously choosing to send the child prayers and good wishes rather than what he described as "the negativity of worrying." While most of us would see that made good sense, it also seems like a big ask. If your child or someone you love is in danger or is unhappy, is it possible *not* to worry?

Only days later I watched as the distinguished Australian writer Kate Grenville was interviewed on television about her novel *The Lieutenant*. She used the idea of worry in a nicely old-fashioned way, describing her drive to "worry away" at the social relationships between Australia's early settlers and the Aboriginal population, as well as their current repercussions, as a "crucial imperative." Using the "worry" word like that usefully broadens its parameters, taking us to a sense of a quiet persistence that won't easily be deflected and may be productive.

Perhaps Kate Grenville's use of the word brings us closer to concern than worry. It is emotionally healthy and natural to be concerned about the people we love, and our work, homes and communities. The pity is that most of us are not *more* concerned about people and events beyond those immediate circles.

But even our most intimate concerns are not emotional or moral only. We are biologically primed to be concerned (and to worry) about our children and those we know and love, not least because the survival of our species depends upon it. One of the many tragedies of some types of drug addiction is that it robs people of this fierce imperative. I will never forget when my own children were babies—a time when I believed that I could hear them breathing in their cribs from rooms away—reading and weeping over clinical accounts of ice and crack-cocaine addicts who gave birth and within hours could literally forget their babies and the care their babies needed.

Some concern, some worry seems to be essential then. So when does it become too much? When does a parent's worry about a child, for example, become intrusive or an additional burden for their child of whatever age? When does worry hamper our efforts to work effectively, maintain a healthy lifestyle or get along with other people?

Worry that feeds on itself—that produces panic, helplessness or despair, rather than insights or solutions—is itself a worry. So is worry that is so fear-driven it adds to others' burdens rather than relieving them. It is helpful and empowering then to know that in most everyday situations we can learn to shift our focus away from repetitive, fearful thinking to a simple and effective version of problem solving—even when there is no specific problem to be solved.

Using our capacities for strategic thinking, planning and problem solving, we are less at risk of being flooded by our emotions, including fear. One of the most helpful questions I have learned to ask is: "What's needed here?" A question like this is essentially calming because it engages different and less primitive functions within the brain than naked fear does.

"I have no idea" may feel like the only possible answer, yet when you persist—actively envisaging how the most capable person you can imagine would deal with this same situation—it is surprising how the mind will supply at least some hint of more encouraging times ahead. It can be even more helpful to write down the question and the answer—almost literally emptying your mind of frightened helplessness and filling it with a sense of a way forward.

A SERIOUS WORRIER'S imagination is often their greatest enemy. So how uplifting it is to find out that the same imagination can become their most powerful ally. The capacity to soothe and reassure ourselves is critical for emotional and physical well-being. Asking "What's needed here?" we are reasserting a sense of control in our inner lives, even when events outside ourselves are frightening or unpredictable.

With just a dash of curiosity and hope, you might discover that even in a tense or troubling situation you have the reservoirs of patience and forbearance that you need. You might discover, simply by going inward (perhaps slowing your breathing as you do so), that you have the capacity to be serenely *present*, letting fear, anxiety and tension go, and letting abundant good wishes arise.

Profound Appreciation

※

Some months ago I spoke to a large group on the theme of encouragement. It's one of my favorite topics and perhaps the most consistent theme underlying my writing. Even the word sounds good to me, and if you are wondering quite what I mean by it, then I believe it can broadly be defined as that vital capacity we all have to lift another person's spirits and bring out the best in them. (We also have the capacity to crush other people's spirits, sometimes with a single cruel or thoughtless remark, or through our silence when a kind word is needed.)

Looking for fresh inspiration, perhaps fresh encouragement, I came across a sentence from pioneering psychologist William James, best known for his 1902 book, *The Varieties of Religious Experience*. Elsewhere, James wrote, "The deepest principle in human nature is the craving to be appreciated."

Is this true for you?

I know that, when I first read this, I walked around with the thought for several days and found it increasingly and fruitfully provocative, not least because of its implication that quietly appreciating our own lives and selves is rarely enough. With few exceptions, we crave to be acknowledged and appreciated by other people, and most of all by those with whom we work or share our lives.

These are the facts: we are social beings; we need one another. And we especially need kindness from one another and the confidence that we matter. James's statement brings that interdependence sharply into focus, particularly once we begin to see ourselves through others' eyes and to wonder what on earth it is we are being appreciated for.

MY HUNCH is that while most of us are delighted when we are appreciated for our actions and achievements, the deep and perhaps unconscious craving that James refers to is for something still more profound. Beyond our rare big moments, beyond whatever prizes or promotions we manage to accumulate, or goals we manage to attain, we *want to be appreciated for ourselves*. We want to be appreciated for our *being*, not just our doing. We want our private, vulnerable self to mean something. That's often what we crave most from those we love: the reassurance of being wholeheartedly and unreservedly accepted.

IN HOPING for appreciation from others, we are forced to recognize that we will never be able to control how or even if other people will express their appreciation toward us. Where we can take charge is in how generously we offer our appreciation and encouragement to other people—and especially those we claim to love.

This must go beyond kind words and gifts, as lovely as they are. If it is even half as important as William James claims, then appreciation, like kindness, needs to become a way of life. Our acts of kindness, good humor and gratitude, our moments of conscious restraint, our willingness to forgive, compromise and tolerate, our confident acceptance that sometimes our agenda will not prevail: these are all ways to express and develop the deepest levels of appreciation that are in our hearts.

They are all ways to say, unceasingly, "You matter."

Perfect Joy

❅

It's always the right time to explore your JQ or joy quotient, a totally unscientific but effective measure of the pleasure and joy you are getting from (and giving to) your everyday life.

Work, and more work, dominates life for many of us. While the lucky ones get at least some pleasure and satisfaction from this, there are many others who simply endure their paid work, or feel so burdened by the sheer volume of all they have to do that they are too depleted even to remember what gives them that glorious sense of being delighted just to be alive.

It is easy enough to say that attitude changes everything, and that even in the busiest of lives a positive attitude toward what we are doing will lift our enjoyment. That is indeed true. But it's not enough. Joy should not only be a by-product of our working lives. We also need times when joy is our focus.

For more than a decade I sang in a gospel class and then a choir. I did it for no reason but joy—pure pleasure—and it sustained me brilliantly through some very tough times. The absurd thing was that I didn't make the time, or find the courage to join that first class until I had cancer. It took that immense jolt to push me in the direction of joy.

The desire to be part of that wonderful choir did eventually pass for me, not least because my interfaith activities took over those needs and others. But my interfaith teaching and ministry are not the same. In my singing days I was responsible for nothing more than turning up enthusiastically and keeping more or less in tune. In my interfaith life I have a leadership role and while that is a privilege and constant learning curve, it also means that I need to continue to create situations where I am still just "one of the crowd."

The seeking of joy (interest, enlightenment) in the company of others is what drives so many people to adult education, group tours, art, craft, sporting and nature interests, as well as to churches or temples. Lasting friendships quickly emerge when people get together around something that is intrinsically uplifting and sustaining. And it is clear from observing how quickly people's mood and well-being lift that this is something almost all of us need, even in a life where it seems there is barely time for family and our older friendships.

Your body is your most accurate barometer when it comes to testing your JQ. When your body feels expansive and relaxed there's little need to ask if you are having a good time! When you feel agitated and tense, or deflated, or when you believe nothing will ever enchant or excite you again, you are in urgent need of greater joy.

Joy is never an intellectual experience only. It can arise from the mind but it will be felt throughout your being. Your senses matter here; so do instinct and imagination.

Other people need not always be involved. Perfect joy can arise in a time of silence and tranquility. There can be moments of pure joy in meditation or simply being. Joy is relaxing, even when you feel stimulated or excited. It is health-giving and sustaining, even in the midst of sorrow or ill health. Joy is appreciative—and it *expresses* appreciation.

Joy restores a sense of proportion. It provides an unequalled chance to reconnect with your own inner resources. It allows a lovely reunion with yourself.

PERSONAL POWER

The Greatest Power

The greatest power we have is to lift the spirits of other people through our choices and behavior—to enhance their lives, and our own.

The greatest responsibility we have is to choose wisely—not just when we feel like it.

The greatest liberty we have is to behave kindly and respectfully without needing a prize or praise—simply because we are free to do so.

The greatest ease we have comes when we can forgive others for their human failings and complexity—and ourselves.

The greatest peace we have is when we can play our vital part in creating harmony between ourselves and other people, regardless of differences.

"I WISH the very best for you" is a significant promise of love. It's one worth keeping.

Love Life Now

＄

Even a long life is brief. Perhaps that's why motivational stories remain so popular. Often the central message they bring is that a brush with death or a hard-won recovery teaches the person how precious life is. Along with that shake-up comes the awareness that life is fragile, hazardous and short. And that each day counts.

We love those stories of transformation. But I wonder if we let ourselves listen to them deeply enough. Do we let ourselves see that such stories describe our own fate also: that they belong to us almost as much as they do to the original storyteller?

It takes a lightning bolt for most of us to come to terms with how fleeting life is and how precious each moment is. Even when we have firsthand experience of a shake-up, we may still live as though we have forever, postponing what matters most. In the immediate wake of a tragedy or brush with death we may tell ourselves that everything will be different. We may make promises to ourselves and to others that are deeply sincere. Yet affirming this gift of life in a sustained way, and letting that conviction guide and direct our daily choices, is often much tougher than it seems.

Over and over again I hear people describing what they would like to do *when* . . . or how they would be living *if only*. . . . I hear that from other people, and sometimes I hear it from myself.

Yet the truth is if we are postponing something that genuinely matters to us, we are betraying life. If we are stuck in a situation that robs us of peace or joy, or are holding on to an ancient bitterness, or are not telling and *showing* the people we love how much we appreciate them, we are betraying life. If we don't know what makes our spirit sing or soar, or what gives our existence meaning, we are betraying life.

WE ARE ALSO betraying life when we believe we have no time to learn forgiveness. And kindness. And appreciation. No time for awe, wonder, bliss, pleasure, delight. No real time for the people we care about. No time to revel in nature, cook for a crowd, read something that inspires us, make something small and beautiful, get together with people unlike ourselves, reconnect with old friends, learn a language, kayak down a wild river or plant a garden whose mature beauty we may never see.

Life, *this* life, is our gift so briefly. Every moment counts.

Open Minds

❀

B arry Marshall and Robin Warren are among my heroes. This is less because they were Nobel Prize winners in medicine in 2005 and more because they are shining examples of that glorious condition called the open mind.

Of course most of us would like to believe we are similarly blessed: open to fresh ideas, eager to see situations objectively rather than subjectively, and ready to shed the limitations of outworn theories. But are we?

DRS. MARSHALL and Warren's brilliance was to resist and transcend assumptions that had hardened into facts. Their medical colleagues worldwide "knew" that stomach ulcers were caused by stress or excess gastric acid. That is what they had been taught. This is what they told patients. This is what they had learned to "see." But was it correct?

Marshall and Warren persistently and stubbornly questioned this assumption. Yet even when they had begun successfully to treat patients with stomach ulcers using antibiotics—following their theory that the ulcers are caused not by stress but by treatable bacteria—many of the scientific minds around them remained closed and defensive.

This is not, we can assume, because those doctors were against medical progress. Nor is it likely that they wished their suffering patients to be anything but well. But, like most of us, they were clearly reluctant to question the certainties that had ruled their thinking. What they had been seeing with such confidence was incorrect. What they had been reporting on and how they had been treating were incorrect. Now they would have to see, understand and treat differently.

A SHIFT like this can be uncomfortable as well as unwelcome. (If we have seen one situation incorrectly, where does it leave us in regard to the rest of our certainties?) Yet it is exactly this ability to go beyond the self-evident that opens the door to new ideas, new conclusions and even new cures as brilliant as Marshall and Warren's.

Like all other disciplines, science relies for progress on inventive, persistent open-mindedness. Yet a great deal of scientific teaching, and certainly much of the practice that flows from it, stultifies this kind of thinking. And the raw curiosity that drives it is frequently disparaged in favor of what is believed to be true.

You AND I are far more likely to suffer stomach ulcers than find a cure for them. But the general lessons about how blinkered even the best intentioned can be apply to all of us.

Only weeks after Marshall and Warren won their prize, I saw an item on television where an experienced naturopath was discussing how he had treated with dietary supplements a four-year-old child's skin irritations and nervous tension. Incidentally, the child's symptoms of autism had noticeably lessened. He was easier to be with and was making better social contact. But when the medical doctor on the show was asked what she thought of this, she could refer only to her own conditioned "seeing": the paradigm upon which she had hung her hat.

She would have used occupational and speech therapy to address the boy's autism, she said. That's fine, too, yet I couldn't help but notice how lacking in curiosity she was about this powerful and touching "secondary gain" from the naturopath's treatment. And how unconsciously disparaging she was of the firsthand observations that both the naturopath and the boy's parents had made.

OPEN-MINDEDNESS, curiosity and a healthy dash of humility are qualities that we would like all our health professionals to have, as well as our scientists, politicians, teachers, media and people of influence. But it is something we could all take up and cultivate to our own advantage. Whether our certainties are religious, economic, scientific, political or psychological, they can easily harden.

However rational we believe ourselves to be, we are led by habits of seeing. As long as we are convinced the earth is flat, we will see evidence of that. As long as we are convinced that the set of answers we already have is the end of the story, we won't look further. Questioning our certainties, opening to a different point of view, listening and observing freshly, or simply assuming that there is always more to know can seem like much to ask. That doesn't make it less urgent, or less essential.

Still Walking

✳

One of the most popular articles I ever wrote in my *Good Weekend* column was on the simple practice of daily walking. I suspect that at least part of that enthusiasm from readers was because I freely confessed to pursuing my fitness goals from an extremely low base! We often love to know that other people are trying things they are not obviously good at—especially when it's in an area where we have our own struggles.

As I look around, I count myself fortunate to have strong legs and functioning joints. Many people of my age, and younger, do not. I am less fortunate with my round shoulders (too many years at the keyboard), neck and arms (ditto), but the reasons why I initially didn't walk for fitness on a frequent basis were emotional rather than physical.

In my first years of motherhood and life in Australia I loved walking with my children. Some of my loveliest memories of their earliest childhood are of walking slowly, slowly, with many stops to gaze, talk and wonder, around our friendly neighborhood and through the large, benignly neglected park we visited almost daily.

When the children grew older I would enjoy striding off to the shops or taking the occasional walk through bush or forests. But taking long walks around city streets purely for the sake of fitness reminded me all too keenly of compulsory walks in my own childhood.

Turning pages in books remained far more attractive than turning corners. But eventually even I reached the point where I could see that the remaining decades of my life would be directly affected by the fitness, strength and flexibility that I committed to develop now.

For several years I walked faithfully. What's more, I grew to love being out walking fast almost every early morning, with walking as its own goal and process. I took pride in how far I could walk and how relatively fast I became. Then, after a few years and perhaps inevitably, my walking program became less ambitious and less regular. Several factors affected me. I changed residence twice (reluctantly) and found those moves physically exhausting. I had some health issues. My work schedule became even more hectic than usual when, in addition to my usual writing and public work, I was also studying and writing my later-life doctoral thesis.

Those demands were not greater than in the previous couple of decades, yet somewhere in the midst of them I told myself that walking to the post office or shops most days was enough. (It isn't.) But those are only details. What changed most was my willingness to put walking—and the time for it—high on my list of priorities. I lost my zest for walking and with it my motivation.

AT ALMOST EVERY STAGE in our lives we can find convincing reasons why we don't have time to do something that benefits us. We can talk ourselves into something and can talk ourselves out of things with just the same levels of conviction. Yet isn't it true that work will always consume as much time as we give it? And that the years of child rearing or caring for others will always be impossibly hectic? What remains true through all our fluctuations of enthusiasm is that even in the most crowded day, time can be found for one of the most crucial investments of all: our own physical and psychological well-being.

What I had to do was recommit. I had to go back to a harder place than my first beginning, once again making my walks a genuine priority.

Just as I had found previously, a regular walk has as many benefits for emotional well-being, sleep, digestion, posture and energy as it has for fitness. But this time around I see even more clearly that I need several factors to sustain me. The most crucial is that I don't give myself a daily choice. Walking is my first activity of each day unless the weather is bleak or I have a genuinely unavoidable appointment.

"Choosing" truly is a waste of emotional effort in this instance. It puts me at the mercy of my feelings and often those feelings tell me that I don't feel like walking and that bottomless piles of work are waiting.

Once I am out the door, however, the pleasures of walking soon kick in. On the days they don't, I walk anyway. I find it also helps to follow a similar route each day that includes some steps, mild hills, city streets and part of a park. Giving myself a literal lift, I wear fabulous, professionally fitted running shoes. And on days that I feel genuinely tired, I allow myself to walk slowly and not as far rather than taking no walk at all.

What matters is that I am out and moving. I can delight in that.

Fewer Things

꙳

Too many recent house and office moves have brought me up hard against my mixed feelings when it comes to shedding possessions or reducing the number of things that fill my cupboards, shelves and life. I know I am not alone in this. As I've talked about it over recent weeks—in increasingly plaintive tones—almost everyone has confessed to having far more possessions than they need or even want. So why do we keep them? Why do we have such difficulty shedding them? And why, in the midst of excess, are we still buying?

MOVING MY country and home many times over a lifetime has convinced me that the reason professional movers appear so dauntingly efficient is less that they display enviable physical strength and more that they are totally unattached to what they should—or perhaps should not—throw into the nearest box.

Precious objects and debris are all the same to them. How different it is when it comes to what we ourselves own, what we once loved or what can still arouse fond memories. Or to things that are truly ghastly but were given to us by a loved one. Or to the countless things that might be needed and are kept "just in case."

The timing of "just in case" is almost laughable. Why is it that we let things sit and age rather than exiling them the moment we see how superfluous they are? Why is something easier to throw out when it's years old rather than new, if it wasn't needed in the first place? This raises so many fascinating questions about the sense of connection we have with what passes through our hands: papers, letters, books, recipes, articles—as well as furnishings, objects and closets full of clothes.

I HAVE CULLED my miles of books several times in recent years and somewhat regret some of what I sold or gave away in the name of efficiency. My library is more than a collection of books to me. It's a history of my reading and writing, my two greatest preoccupations. In many ways it is a history of my most personal self. But like most parents, my greatest throw-out reluctance comes up around things that relate to my children's early years.

My children—both now in their twenties and not children any longer—show few signs of sentimentality about those carefully preserved paintings, sculptures, writings, notes and photos that fill boxes and cupboards. Yet I know that they are glad these items still exist. And for me those things are powerful memory-carriers.

Quite unexpectedly during one of my moves I found a little pad where I had written rather stern notes during my children's adolescence, making suggestions about what household tasks they might like to divide and conquer before my return a few hours later. Some were clearly written in exasperation. Now I reread them, feeling touched for us all.

THERE ARE FEWER convincing reasons why I still have tiny clothes from my skinny-young-woman years in London. Or so many clothes that are relatively new but drearily similar. How many pairs of plain black trousers and generous cover-up garments does any woman need?

"I am going to buy nothing but books and perishables for a year," I said firmly to a friend. Which then caused us to reminisce about the days when people could fit all their clothes into tiny free-standing wooden wardrobes, and when the kind of built-ins and walk-in closets that we now take for granted represented a level of glamour and also acquisitiveness that belonged in the movies but not real life.

Mine may be the last generation to be raised with the quaint notion that frugality and "making do" are virtues. Like most of my contemporaries, I have taken to conspicuous consumption enthusiastically but ineffectively. When new things are justified, I still feel compelled to find a good home for the older versions.

HOWEVER I DISGUISE and organize them, too many objects fill my life. But oh, some do turn out to be newly useful! Suddenly I am proud again of having kept so many of my children's books. And that I can provide the new, beloved children in my life with an instant library of fondly remembered treasures. I am also delighted that I still have enough Legos, wooden toys and blocks for hours of play. I am not quite sure what to do with old manuscripts of my books, paintings and prints of minor value that have not been hung for years, occasional lamps that work but for which I will never find another occasion, or furniture that has traveled with me through all these moves and that now looks more elderly than I do.

Perhaps my greatest discovery during this latest move was confirmation that when things are imbued with personal history and real feeling, however modest they are, they remain valuable. When they are simply "things," however costly, they are expendable. It's worth a move to see that.

Empty Time?

✹

"No time" may seem to be the cliché of our time. And for many people it reflects a painful truth. No matter how fast we run, our in-box is never empty, friends and extended family remain neglected, and the life we want to live is always out of reach. But it can be just as painful—maybe more so—to have too little to do and days that stretch ahead that are unstructured and empty.

What people share in both those situations is a sense of powerlessness. The person who has too little to do, however, is often additionally struggling with feelings of uselessness or even shame. Being constantly busy is a way of life that may cost us dearly. Nevertheless, it is widely applauded, while *not* being busy can be extremely confronting.

Who are we when we are not defined by other people's needs or demands? Or by an agenda set by someone else? Who are we when we no longer have a shorthand "role" by which to describe ourselves, our interests, our place in the world?

It's no surprise that many people who find themselves with "all the time in the world" feel dismayed or daunted rather than exhilarated. And while this is generally worse when they didn't choose their circumstances—when a job is terminated early or a relationship comes to an end—it can also be tough for people who have stepped voluntarily into a new life but have yet to adjust to it.

Adjusting to any new life stage takes a good deal of emotional and mental energy. None of us has much of that when our mood is low or we feel powerless or depressed. Other people's expectations can unwittingly intensify the problem. If we believe we ought to be enjoying our time and freedom, it can be even more confronting when what we miss most are routines that are not of our own making and external demands that we must race to meet.

Those external demands do more than give us outer structure. They also make us feel secure internally. Problem solving, meeting our daily challenges and working socially and cooperatively underpin emotional health. For most of us, the easiest way to find those benefits is through our personal relationships (friendships, romantic relationships, community), and also from our paid work.

This makes it extremely serious that even in countries as rich as ours we apparently take it as inevitable that some citizens will never have paid work, and will never have the structure, sense of purpose and self-respect that work gives. Just as concerning is the assumption that in pursuit of so-called economic rationalism many people will lose their chance to work, while those left behind may find themselves drowning in work's demands. (Not too much rationality there.)

WHILE WE CANNOT always influence or change our outer circumstances, we can nevertheless change the way we think about ourselves and value our lives and social contributions. Alongside the grim statistic that the majority of retirees are unprepared for the changes that retirement brings is the more uplifting statistic that one of the happiest groups generally in Western societies are *active* retirees. These are the people who are still learning, formally or informally. They make it their business to be engaged with people and interests beyond themselves, and they maintain a sense of outer purpose that works for them inwardly also.

IF YOU ARE young and jobless, or middle-aged and facing the agonies of retrenchment, or if you have given everything to a family that has grown into independence and no longer needs you, or if you are one of the many people who feel fine through the working week but desolate at weekends, then the cheerful purposefulness of those most active and engaged retirees can seem hard to take. But there is something to be learned here.

The truth is, we are social beings with hungry minds. To enjoy life, we must engage with it. When a purposeful life is not on offer from the outside, we must create one. How we do this will very much reflect our interests, aptitudes and emotional courage. Accepting that challenge may be one of the hardest things we will ever need to do. We may need help. We may need to learn new ways of accepting help as well as giving it. That, too, may require a tough adjustment. But in expanding our sense of the possible in these ways, we will create a new way of living that may be unexpectedly rewarding.

Going Greener

✧

Some weeks ago I received an invitation to "go green" with my electricity and gas bills. This couldn't have arrived at a better time. I was already turning over in my mind the conviction that the most serious global warnings are not serious enough. Along with that, I had been wondering why so many of us who know what we should and could be doing to help the physical world on which we entirely depend are, nevertheless, *not acting quickly or wisely*.

Self-confidence surely depends upon our ability to see what's needed in the wider world as well as in our own personal environment—and to contribute in the best way that we can. Each of us will do this differently. Some will give money to causes. Some will take a leadership or activist role. Some will make it their business to be better informed. Others will take up the challenge purely through the way they live and how they accommodate the new awareness that what we most take for granted has a finite life.

EVEN WITH the best of intentions, however, the simplest things can seem too much: using energy-efficient lightbulbs, showerheads and appliances; choosing hardier, less water-needy plants; faithfully composting; avoiding plastic bags and excessive packaging; shop-ping far less; taking brief showers only; walking when possible and using public transport; recycling; avoiding excessive heating and air-conditioning; choosing fuel-efficient cars; shunning toxic products or those from nonrenewable sources.

None of those measures seriously inconveniences us. None is new or startling. Yet the fact is, most of us—good, well-intentioned people who care about the world in which we live as well as one another—are not taking nearly enough responsibility for the cli-mate, the soil, rivers and oceans, the air or even the sliver of world that is our own backyard.

Government and business can get away with continuing to harm the environment and doing far too little to heal it only because *we as individuals are also highly ambivalent about what we can and should be doing.* This can't be because we don't know what to do. We do. And it can't be because we don't care. We do. But still there is a missing link in too many lives between "knowing" and acting wisely.

I FEEL increasingly impatient with the usual excuses: that our changes won't make a significant difference; that the science of climate change is over- or under-reported; that the situation in the third world is so frightful that our own demands might as well continue unchecked. Or that it is simply too hard for busy people to change their entrenched habits of behavior and thinking.

This last excuse is possibly the least convincing, in part because it is precisely where the most effective changes *can* take place. But only if we want that.

Switching to a more environmentally friendly way of living is much less difficult than giving up smoking, for example. Yet the smoking culture, and our tolerance of it, has changed in ways that would have seemed extremely optimistic twenty years ago.

Some people do continue to smoke even into their dying years. And far too many young people still smoke. But the social constraints around smoking, together with a wider understanding of the health hazards, have combined to make smoking far less acceptable and appealing.

Perhaps that potent combination of social pressure, education and personal responsibility has not yet kicked in with environmental issues. We may not be encouraging one another sufficiently. We may not be talking about the issues constructively enough. We may not even be frightened enough.

I WONDER, too, if our concerns about what's "enough" are not themselves debilitating? Some people I've talked to say frankly that any contribution they could make would be too small to matter. Switching off a few lights, giving up routine meat eating, walking or catching a bus and leaving your car at home, planting trees, saving water, buying organic food and reusing plastic bags: these small and most obvious steps may seem paltry or even self-serving in the face of a possible catastrophe. Yet the truth is that *it is as individuals that we have littered, poisoned and used up our world.* It is also as individuals—cheering one another on—that we can turn the tide.

Sorting Mountains
from Molehills

Even in the best-ordered lives people make mistakes, misjudge situations, say what they shouldn't and don't do what they should. At least, I assume that's true because, to be frank, I have never experienced a "best-ordered" life, and probably never will.

Doing too much is my downfall. It means I do, indeed, get a great deal done. But, like most people, my levels of achievement are patchy. I am patient and passionate when it comes to my writing but am far less sanguine when it comes to the torrent of administration that surrounds my writing life. The great promise that computers would save us from having an office filled with paper was clearly false. We now have more paper (and demands) and not less. This is in part because we increasingly worship work. It's also because instant communications seem to demand instant responses.

WHEN WE ARE WORKING FAST as well as hard, mistakes are inevitable. How we contemplate those mistakes—whether we call them calamities or take them in our stride—will have a significant effect on our capacity to enjoy our days and years, rather than enduring them.

Some years ago self-help writer Richard Carlson came up with a series of books called *Don't Sweat the Small Stuff.* More than offering just a smart marketing idea, Carlson was pointing out that mistakes happen, inconveniences abound, agendas clash—and that we should fret and "sweat" only when the issue truly warrants it. Most issues don't. The trick is, of course, to know how to sort the big from the small.

"WILL THIS MATTER a day from now—or in a week?" is a good place to start. "Is this hurting someone—or just my pride?" is also helpful. "What needs to be done next?" takes us forward out of the mire. It also lets us breathe easier.

Much of the "stuff" that worries us is transitory rather than tragic. When we stop to think (itself a blessing), it's rarely sufficient reason to ruin a day. Many of our "errors" are slips or inconveniences, nothing more. The mistakes that do matter are those that hurt or betray other people, rather than irritating them.

Forgetting something important to someone else, saying something cruel or threatening, overlooking someone's feelings even when you didn't mean to, being dishonest or disrespectful: that warrants a good deal of "sweating" and change of tactic. It may also require humility on your part to ask for forgiveness. And a clear resolution that such a mistake will not be repeated.

You may be in more trouble still if you care too little than if you care too much. But caring too much, or too indiscriminately, is inefficient and exhausting.

. . .

WE ALL NEED to know when it's a molehill we are fussing about rather than a mountain. To do that it helps to notice more broadly what makes your heart race, what stories you are telling yourself about what you can and can't achieve, how *entitled* you feel to fuss, and how your reactions and responses are affecting the people around you.

It's often in other people's eyes that we most fear appearing stupid, careless or insignificant. So how comforting it is to remember that when we deal with those inevitable slips with at least some self-awareness and grace, we grow in others' esteem—and in our own.

Choosing—and Recovering

✣

Choosing is something I have written about often, not least in *Choosing Happiness* where choosing is as vital a topic as happiness is.

Choosing is a highly significant act of self-determination. The more consciously we can do it, the more stable we will feel inwardly. This doesn't mean that all our choices will be right. Or that we are not constantly impacted by other people's choices. But when we feel at least reasonably in charge of how and what we are choosing, this will reflect an inward steadiness and sense of safety that can only be enhanced as our sense of agency and self-responsibility grows.

BLAMING OTHER PEOPLE for how our life is turning out, or because the dog or baby has thrown up on the new carpet, or because we sent a report to the printer with a glaring error, strips us of our personal power. It also takes us into an emotional pit of our own making. As our choices accumulate, they are literally shaping the person we are becoming. But there are many ways in which the notion of choice is much less clear-cut.

Politicians and people alike, for example, talk a great deal about choice in education, employment and health, as though choice itself were an equal access opportunity. Questions of choice become more complicated still in situations that are not dependent on wealth or health but on quirks of fate or luck. Losing a job you need because the company collapses; not having the marriage or career you had always expected; not having the child you've longed for since you were a child yourself; buying a house in the wrong suburb at the wrong time; having a major crisis of meaning or faith; losing a beloved person far too early; experiencing betrayal: the list can be endless. And seem endlessly unfair.

Where, then, does choice play its part?

Serious loss, disappointment, sorrow or regret is always felt acutely. And knowing that others may have even worse sorrows brings little comfort.

VIKTOR FRANKL is one of my heroes. Author of *Man's Search for Meaning*, among other books, Holocaust survivor, philosopher, psychiatrist and writer, Frankl urges us to take up the challenging thought that when we can't change a difficult or unwelcome situation we are forced to change ourselves.

Perhaps what he means is that we must *change our vision of what's possible* so that we can more courageously believe in our capacity to recover and move back into life, *no matter how life has changed*.

Perhaps he would also want us to examine what we believe our entitlements are in this life. And whether an overwhelming sense of outrage is adding to our sorrows. We may not want to see this. It could feel just as impossible as changing what has already happened. What Frankl is pointing to, though, is that it is in our way of seeing and interpreting events—how we describe them to ourselves and especially how we describe our capacity to accept and deal with them—that we have some choice, however tenuous that feels.

IT IS IMPOSSIBLE to offer a simple formula for recovery in any stark situation. What I do know, though, is that talking about what we are feeling is almost always much better than avoiding it. It's better too than pretending that we are feeling all right when, plainly, we are not.

I also know that when two or more people are sharing a loss, they need to be extremely cautious about blaming one another or judging one another if they mourn or grieve differently. While burying our grief or fears in a mountain of work or at the bottom of a glass is tempting, it gives us no chance to heal. Some people will collapse in the face of a loss; others will redouble their activities, at least for a while.

IT TAKES COURAGE to speak up frankly about our toughest losses. It takes more courage still to accept care from others, especially when that's often clumsy and inadequate. Yet we are social creatures and while sharing our sorrows cannot change them it may reestablish a crucial sense of connection with life beyond ourselves. It may also lead to the possibility of supporting others in a similar situation.

This requires opening to at least some acceptance of what can't be changed. In those starkest moments sometimes a different idea of choice and even unexpected possibilities may emerge.

But first there needs to be honest grieving for the old reality or lost dreams. Recovery from any kind of serious setback is usually patchy and often far from complete. ("Closure" is often a mirage, and may even impede our eventual acceptance of profound changes, inward and outward.)

Patience as well as time is needed, and also openness, because even the toughest of situations can yield up moments of kindness and relief if we let them.

It's KINDNESS to ourselves, and kindness from other people, that can sustain and restore trust: not trust that life will be as we once hoped, but trust that life is nevertheless worth living—and that our own crumpled version of it remains precious and unique.

When "Sorry" Is Not Enough

✺

S orry" is a powerful word. It carries an emotional force that can be life changing. Yet when it comes to healing serious hurt or conflict, saying sorry is rarely enough.

An apology—or simple expression of sorrow or regret—has its greatest power when someone unreservedly acknowledges the harm they have caused *and* owns up to how this has hurt other people. To admit "I caused this" is genuinely confronting. It can take a long time and much backsliding to get to that point.

Making excuses, looking for both sides of the story, feeling resentful that you have been caught out or self-pitying because your dignity is now sullied, or apologizing to get yourself out of trouble or to look good are all quite different responses from recognizing the harm you have done and genuinely regretting its effect on others' lives.

A meaningful apology is unconditional. It leaves excuses behind. It emerges from a willingness to take full responsibility for your actions. But even that is not enough. It must also be based upon *an*

unconditional resolve not to cause that same or similar pain again. Fear
of losing other people's love and respect, outbursts of self-pity or
panic, or convoluted rationalizations are common responses that
are essentially self-focused. They are about you, not those you have
hurt. So is even a faint hope that you might get away with it next
time. To make a change in behavior effective, your focus needs to
switch from yourself to those you have injured. You need to comprehend at the deepest possible level what power you have to hurt
or heal. That power, and how you wield it, has to be your most
serious concern and focus.

WITHOUT SEEKING THEM OUT, I have heard several painful
stories lately of people who are fluent in the language of apology but
seemingly unable to make real change to their behavior. While each
story is different, that awful sense of "Here we go again" is much
the same. In one situation a husband has been having brief, meaningless affairs for years—or perhaps not so meaningless, as he
doesn't stop them. In another situation, a middle-aged daughter's
intermittent but catastrophic gambling leaves her elderly parents
feeling betrayed as well as far poorer. In a third situation, a woman
who still cares very much about her partner is having to face leaving
him because their children are now as anxious as she is about when
their dad will next "lose it" and become a raging, unreachable
monster.

CONVENTIONAL psychological thinking pushes people to find
reasons why they or their loved ones are behaving badly: terrible

parents or parents who were too kind; too much money or too little; poor self-image or excessive ego; too much stress or too little. Almost any scenario will do.

Some factors *are* significant. We don't enter or move through life with equal gifts or insights. Sometimes the agonies in our lives do pile up at an unbearable rate. But "reasons why" can also be distracting.

The primary cause of behavior that hurts other people is seldom in the past. The past matters, but less than the way someone thinks about themselves and other people right now in the present moment.

The husband, daughter and father in those stories all see themselves as the victims of their behavior or history. In the apology phases, they will acknowledge with regret the hurt they are causing. But this apology remains shallow. The suffering they are causing others is less urgent for them than their own emotions and needs. Until they understand and reverse that, whatever sorrow they may feel for the pain they are causing will remain muted and ineffective.

WAKING UP to our power to harm—or uplift—others is crucial to gaining emotional maturity. We are not victims of our past. We are not slaves to our most familiar feelings. Our feelings and history shape and influence us. But they needn't hold us back.

When our reasons to do so are resolute enough, we can behave and respond differently. This is the only way out of terminal egocentricity. It is also the only way toward lasting self-respect.

A shift in priorities as big as this one is profoundly challenging. It calls on our highest levels of persistence, courage and integrity.

It asks nothing less than that we take unconditional responsibility for the effect of *all* our choices and actions on other people. This is radical. Yet it is one of the purest expressions of kindness known to humankind. It will change not just the well-being of those around us, but also how we perceive, value and trust ourselves.

Family First?

❋

We increasingly take it for granted that people can and should leave dangerous or loveless intimate relationships. There are still not nearly enough support systems in place for people to leave situations of domestic violence and abuse, but the cultural shifts on that issue—so that the victim is no longer blamed—are immensely significant.

At the same time, though, many of us believe that we ought to get along with our biological family, no matter how difficult, demanding or abusive those individuals may be.

You might have a granny whose political views threaten your blood pressure or an uncle who is numbingly intolerant or self-absorbed. But that may be a rare irritation as well as a trivial one. The situation is far more confronting if you seriously dislike or fear one of your parents. Or if it is one of your siblings whose violent outbursts terrify you. And it may be most tragic of all if you are the parent of an adult child who controls, frightens or threatens you.

OVER THE YEARS of leading workshops and support groups, I have often found myself talking with people about what it might mean to spend less time with anyone who routinely upsets or frightens them, regardless of how closely they are related. "Putting yourself first" sounds like an impossible goal for some. Even the idea of taking better care of yourself can seem virtually incomprehensible until there's a major crisis. Yet if someone routinely puts you down or spends their time with you attacking, complaining, drinking excessively or taking drugs, or being aggressive or critical, this will have a powerful negative effect on your health, your self-confidence and your most fundamental sense of self.

In fact, this is the kind of situation where those crucial mind–body–emotion links are most obvious. You have only to think about how physically tense you feel around someone who hurts or frightens you and, conversely, how relaxed you feel with someone you love and trust.

Nevertheless, it remains all too easy to override whatever messages your body is sending. You may feel literally ill in the company of someone you are supposed to care about—head aching as much as heart—yet helpless to change the situation.

This is in part because the belief is deep in most of us that families should tolerate and accept one another, no matter what. This means that if people do give up on a close relationship, they often experience far more complicated feelings of grief and devastation than when a more loving and mutual relationship ends in death.

BECAUSE THE SITUATION is complex, my sense is strong that there is no single right way to go forward other than knowing that *you have a right and a responsibility to take care of yourself.*

This doesn't always mean cutting the person out of your life entirely. It is often better to face up to the difficulties honestly, reduce your expectations, silence your excuses for them, and strictly limit the time you spend with that person, *ensuring that someone you can trust is always present.*

It also helps to dilute the effects of those debilitating times by spending far more time with people who are capable of being loving, cheerful and supportive. And what's more broadly uplifting is to take on board the idea that you can afford to be kind to yourself—and that this need not harm the other person.

Tolerating intolerable behavior benefits no one. It fails to set the boundaries that the person cannot set for him- or herself. It reduces your self-respect. And, frankly, it drains your life of vitality and pleasure.

"Failure" in any of our closest relationships is a difficult burden to bear. This pain is worsened when most of the changes must come from one side. Hope for any significant transformation may be scant. This means that when a situation has come to feel unceasingly bleak, any small, subtle changes you can identify and put in place will be of real value. Simply exercising a greater sense of choice, and doing this with renewed kindness and less fear, can at least restore some sense of confidence, trust and calm.

I know through my own experience of the very toughest times in my life, some of which seemed as though they would never end, that when we feel inadequate or perhaps helpless to change a situation or to help someone else, it can take considerable courage to claim any right to help ourselves. But that's just the time when we must make such a claim. Discovering that we can rediscover kindness and self-care as a genuine resource even and especially in those unrelenting times, life begins once again to feel a good deal sweeter.

Childhood Shadows

※

None of us comes to our relationships unencumbered by the emotional climate in which we grew up. Many people who were raised in a household dominated by a parent's dark or withdrawn moods, or by their rages or unhappiness, will find themselves in similar situations in their adult relationships—despite their best intentions. They may resent this. They may find it hard to believe. Yet, here they are.

My experience is that in this situation many otherwise confident people will feel deeply confused about their rights as an adult to assert their own needs for a more peaceful, respectful way of living. Some will question their innate value as a human being. Shame and fear will get in the way, and especially the childhood fear that nothing they can do will make things better.

ANGRY PEOPLE often blame others for their misery or aggression. They may not do this consciously, but each time their anger flares, or their irritability shows, or they withdraw into a deep unhappiness, blame is felt.

The person on the receiving end may know that this is unjust and unfair, yet it is difficult to shake off entirely all sense of responsibility. Children are intensely vulnerable to their parents' moods. They have no equal power to exert and they have no way to escape. When the emotional climate in a child's home is tense and confusing, learning to be direct about your needs becomes extremely difficult. It's like a language that you've barely learned. And the multiple languages of anxiety become all too familiar.

MOODY, DIFFICULT people almost certainly believe that they can't control their moods. But whatever they consciously believe, they undoubtedly control the reactions and even the perceptions of everyone around them. This doesn't benefit them. And it certainly doesn't benefit their family members.

Pretending that things are all right when they are not, family members often find it difficult to develop the clarity and even the self-respect that they need to make their own psychologically healthy choices—especially when it comes to intimate relationships. They often lack the confidence to assert themselves appropriately. This makes them vulnerable. They may become overly assertive, even aggressive, as a way of coping; they may become withdrawn or even helpless. Some will, of course, perpetuate the very patterns they want to escape. But that is certainly not inevitable.

IF YOU GREW UP in a family where either or both of your parents were tense, angry, drug- or alcohol-dependent or emotionally unpredictable you may have become oversensitive to your own moods and other people's, without recognizing the choices, capacities and the *right* you have to take good care of yourself.

You may find it much easier to take care of other people, rather than yourself. Some of your own reactions and especially your occasional outbursts or times of depression may confuse you. Perhaps you have become a professional rescuer (working in the helping professions). Perhaps you are the good friend other people routinely turn to. But this does not necessarily make it easier to see when you need to rescue yourself.

For you, the challenge may be to discover greater pleasure and security in your own existence and a much stronger sense that you are entitled to assert your needs without feeling that you are dominating other people or taking something from them. This may first mean learning to recognize which of your emotional patterns and responses reflect fear or anxiety and especially the need to placate other people. It might mean noticing when you are discounting your own needs or feelings. Or perhaps feeling swamped by them. It can also mean checking on any tendency to be a martyr: "Everyone's agenda matters more than mine . . . someone has to do it. . . ."

It could also mean sometimes consciously asking, "What do I most want at this time or in this situation?" Writing this question down in your journal is almost absurdly helpful, especially when you make the time to return to it more than once, as old insights give way to new. It could also mean being much clearer about what you *don't* want to put up with or make excuses for. And it could mean taking the time *to seek more positive situations and experiences and to feel entitled to do so.*

Acting on this newfound clarity will require courage. But this leads to seeing that the past need not overwhelm the present. And that the present and the future are, at least somewhat, yours to create.

Adult Carers, Childhood Grief

✺

Suffering takes a huge toll on many people's lives. But often the people supporting those who are suffering are also under tremendous stress.

It may be that your loved one has a chronic illness, or a disability that can only worsen. Perhaps they have lost a job and can't find another. Or they have been treated unfairly. Perhaps someone is struggling to find love or meaning. Perhaps they are causing harm through their own choices or behaviors. Or they can't find the strength to leave a relationship that is undermining or dangerous.

There's no point comparing levels of suffering in these common scenarios. What we do know is that it can be overwhelming for a loving bystander to feel useless in the face of a loved one's pain. The instinct to heal, shield, uplift and make everything all right for the people we love is as healthy as it is powerful. It's what allows us to transcend selfishness and self-interest. It can sustain astounding levels of devotion and care over years, even decades. But when it seems impossible to help effectively, the pain of that can be intense. Those feelings of helplessness are themselves confronting. When they meet and mock the instinct to save our loved ones, it can feel unbearable.

. . .

IN MY YEARS of working with people around these kinds of issues I have noticed two patterns that seem to make this kind of situation even harder. The first is when our help is refused. There can be legitimate reasons for this. Sometimes what is offered is perceived to be controlling or intrusive. Or perhaps the person we want to help finds being helped unbearable. The loving bystander then has to deal with horrible feelings of rejection on top of the concern and pain they already feel.

That's a story that can be dramatically eased with better communication, clarifying what is wanted as well as what is being offered and why. Professional counseling can work wonders in these circumstances, clarifying and healing a troubled situation so that each person involved can feel validated and then can relieve rather than worsen the initial difficulties.

The other situation when helplessness seems to feel particularly unbearable is when someone is allowed to help, and does everything they can, yet still feels overwhelmed and in danger of sleeplessness, loss of vitality, increased anxiety or clinical depression.

When the reactions seem extreme to us, there may well be a long history for the would-be helper of being a bystander to suffering and being unable to relieve it. Sometimes this stretches back to childhood. Perhaps the person had a parent or sibling who had a chronic or terminal illness. Perhaps they had a drug- or alcohol-addicted sibling. Perhaps their family circumstances changed abruptly for the worse when money was lost or a parent left.

Surviving those experiences may have given that adult what seemed like exceptional emotional resilience. Yet in a new situation of attempting to care for someone they love—a situation that may superficially appear to be quite different—the intensity of child-hood helplessness and grief can return.

IT IS EASY, as adults, to ignore how children can simultaneously feel dependent on their caretakers yet responsible for what's going on around them. Because it is so clear to the adults that whatever is happening in the family constellation more generally is *not* the child's fault or responsibility, it is easy to overlook the pain and even failure and shame that children can and do feel in such situations. Children will generally articulate those feelings only with support and help. Often in the midst of that widespread crisis, getting such help is not on the agenda.

It may not be until decades later when an adult reexperiences anxiety and helplessness, as well as the distress of someone else's pain, that it becomes clearer what is long buried. Likening this to post-traumatic stress may not be an overstatement in many situations. Understanding the origin of those feelings may provide the first glimpses of relief in what's already a demanding situation.

ANYONE WHO is in a long-term supporting role must find ways to value what they are doing, rather than dwelling too obsessively on what cannot be done. Without this, exhaustion will be far greater. Carers also need care. Supporters also need support. This means that if we are in such a situation we must make life as rewarding and even pleasurable as we can.

While someone we love is suffering, our own needs can seem irrelevant. Even without the family history complications I have observed, many people need help to disentangle complex emotions and to reclaim some basic sense of what they can still have or enjoy, never mind "deserve." They may need help, too, to discover how to receive comfort and support, as well as give it. But I am confident in saying that taking these small, significant measures is helpful all around. At least to some extent they may protect the carer from emotional as well as physical fatigue. They may also save the person being cared for from additional stress, guilt or grief.

SELF-CONFIDENCE

Speaking Up

In Our Own Time

Open to Beauty

A Weight Off Your Mind

Your Own Best Expert

Make Up Your Own Mind

The Almost Perfect Ego

Surviving the Global Stress Crisis

Check Your Assumptions (They May Be Wrong)

Speaking Up

✿

I'll confess to being a fairly opinionated person. And I am perfectly aware how fortunate I am that exploring the human condition in books like this one, as well as in a stimulating variety of articles and talks, gives me exceptional opportunities not just to express my opinions but, better still, to review and renew them.

Being curious and incipiently opinionated was far more difficult for me as a child. Finding your own voice, formulating opinions and then testing them, is crucial for people of all ages but it's particularly essential for young people as they emerge into adulthood. In the far less permissive days of my childhood and adolescence, offering an original opinion was largely disallowed, particularly at school. I'm talking about the dark ages of the 1960s, when pupils (not yet "students") were widely encouraged to be silently cooperative. What this meant was that being good and deserving of praise depended on your willingness and eagerness to conform. If you were invited to express an opinion, it was assumed that this would be a bland regurgitation of what others thought and taught. Anything else was simply wrong.

. . .

OUR SELF-CONFIDENCE remains in hibernation until we can trust the complex cognitive and emotional processes involved in sorting out what we think. And then finding the confidence and voice to express it.

Where we are most likely to get into trouble is if we believe there is only one opinion worth taking seriously (ours, naturally!). Or when we feel so attached to our opinions that if someone disagrees with us or holds a differing point of view, we feel personally undermined or insulted.

One of the great benefits I have experienced in getting older is that I am far less attached to most of my opinions than I once was. This doesn't mean that I care any less than I once did, but I am certainly less driven to try to persuade others to see things the way that I do. I am no longer, I hope, a zealot pursuing my broadly feminist/social justice agenda with missionary zeal! Nevertheless, my commitment to tolerance doesn't mean tolerating or colluding with what causes harm. And even now there are times when I feel as compelled as I ever did to speak up, however uncomfortable or exposed it makes me feel.

VIOLENCE PASSING as entertainment; religious, gender and racial bigotry; petty cruelty; neglect and abuse of children; indifference to the fate of our planet and the most vulnerable: these are all areas where I find it impossible to be silent. I have also been a committed pacifist throughout my adult life. In fact, while my political and religious affiliations have changed somewhat, my pacifism has been a constant. This is a more complex position than simply calling for an end to war. It questions violence as an acceptable solution to *any* personal, national or international problem. And it certainly questions violence as an acceptable or desired first resort.

IT WILL COME as no surprise that I continue to have a strong commitment to gender and racial justice. But it's those pacifist views that have got me into far more trouble over the years, especially with people who believe violence is inevitable and defensible.

In one instance, someone was so incensed by an opinion piece I wrote for a major newspaper that he sent a deluge of quite mad letters not simply objecting to my views but threatening retribution. The double irony of this will be obvious. First, that my opinions about peace, of all topics, should have so enraged him; second, that he—like many of us—so strongly identified with his own opinions that he felt attacked and insulted by my different viewpoint and was driven to attack in return.

A GROWN-UP VIEW of our own opinions would see us shaking them out and auditing them on a regular basis. Some of the opinions that we have had "forever" might no longer serve us—or anyone else—well. Some of them might not be our own opinions at all but something we picked up from hyper-opinionated commentators on radio or television, or because it's what "people like us" invariably think.

For opinions to count they need to be owned—but not too fiercely. It's a truism that most people become more fixed and defensive and narrower in their opinions as they age. But the older people I know who are most alive are also clear-minded and open-minded.

They care a lot. They think a lot. They do know right from wrong. They aren't afraid to be challenged. They aren't afraid to listen to opinions as well as offer them. They aren't afraid to change their minds—or have their minds changed, by new thoughts, new stimulation and (best of all) new experiences, wisdom and insights.

In Our Own Time

✿

We all know how slippery our perceptions of time can be: how a few minutes can become a lifetime while we wait for significant news and how hours can become seconds when we are thoroughly absorbed. We also know that we often think about and describe time as a currency. We spend it. We waste it. We use it. It uses us.

Few of us think about time without some misgivings. Perhaps that's in part because our difficulties with it reflect our more fundamental concerns with how we are shaping our lives, as well as the underlying realization that time will, for all of us, eventually run out.

This makes it more poignant still when we feel used up by time rather than using it in the ways that we would most like. That familiar state of mind was intensified for me recently, not least because I had ten precious days to "spend" with "all the time in the world."

I can't even remember when I last went away without books squarely directed toward my current research, without a laptop, without a stimulating environment that begged to be explored and—crucially—without family responsibilities or, indeed, responsibilities to anyone but myself. For those ten days time existed only to be filled or emptied or ignored: not to push me where I didn't want to go.

OF COURSE (*of course!*) I did have some goals. I wanted to explore the extent to which I could detach from my everyday habits of activity (more easily each day). I wanted to discover how much sleep I need in order not to feel the least bit tired (quite a bit more than my usual six hours). I was curious, too, to find out where my creative daydreaming would take me when the day was not chopped into pieces by overlapping demands.

MY CHILDREN are independent now. I have the usual household tasks and domestic life to see to and am fortunate enough to see my children and other family members and dear friends often. (And how precious that is.) But the urgent domestic demands that once directed my time are now virtually nonexistent. Without the children to be thinking of morning, noon and through the night, I am more rather than less aware that I am virtually as busy as I ever was. In fact, without consciously choosing this, I seem to have simply increased my paid and voluntary workload. Time still all too rarely feels my own.

I'm conscious of the ironies implicit in this confession. Do I *manage* time as I should or could? I am also aware, with some frustration, that many of you reading this may perceive the life of a writer as essentially contemplative, perhaps even placid and dreamy. And surely that would be even more so when the writer in question (me) writes about what the poet Rainer Maria Rilke calls "the deepest things"?

But for all that it beckons like an oasis, that quiet ease behind a closed door is not a life I have been able to achieve. My nature and personality certainly do allow me the deep focus and absolute concentration that writing demands. In fact, that focus sustains me through all the more hectic, externally directed times. I am also capable of holding on to that essential connection over a number of years as I weave whatever my current writing project is with other more immediate demands (teaching, talks, freelance journalism, raising children) in the past. At the same time, I am painfully aware how much of my time is spent attending to the many activities that support or surround my writing, rather than on writing itself.

Some of that is advantageous. Having to leave my desk in order to supplement my writing income keeps me in touch with a huge variety of people and their concerns. It also reminds me how intrinsically unrewarding a great deal of desk-based administration work is: work that is everything for many people. I remain lucky that it is part of my work life and not all of it. And yet, I again confess, as I get older I resent more rather than less the constancy of being my own reluctant admin assistant so much of the time.

TAKING THOSE ten days off, taking time out in a small town that was pretty enough but wonderfully *un*stimulating, I had nothing to do but read for pleasure, walk, meditate, cook a little, dream, and rest a lot. Doing that, and with only my own agenda to consider, I rediscovered the spaciousness of time: that time truly is coexistent with timelessness, with eternity. I also discovered how often I remain enslaved to time, haunting my own self with all those slave terms: "must," "ought," "have to," "should."

. . .

THIS DELIGHT in time's spaciousness doesn't mean that I am ready yet to walk away from work. And that's just as well, given I will need to be at my desk in some form or other until the last possible moment. What it did mean is that I took ten days' respite from being *busy*, from being *responsible*, from being *responsive* to the demands of work and other people's timetables and agenda.

I took time. I took my own time.

And in the absence of any sense of urgency or inner pressure, I relished the sensuality that time could allow me. Over several days I relished raking a mountain of fallen leaves. I loved smelling the rose face cream as I applied it to my face after my morning shower. I noticed how comfortable it was to feel sanguine rather than harried when the line in the coffee shop ground to a halt. I was able to listen deeply to music rather than relegating it to the background. I was waking and praying and walking when I felt like it and not when the alarm rang. When friends and family rang to chat, I could listen wholeheartedly without regard for the clock.

For once, I didn't have to wrestle time, push against time, or push through it. I could listen to my body's and soul's needs rather than overriding them. It's true I did find myself thinking about work—but only about its depths and rewards, not its demands.

A GREAT DEAL of what I rediscovered was not about time at all, but attitude. There are some circumstances (and falling in love is one) when we suddenly discover that we have all the time in the world. So I suspect that many of our more routine responses are

determined by habit, restlessness or anxiety rather than unrelenting need.

TIME IS ALSO a need. A sense of inner spaciousness is a need. Yet
those needs are routinely sacrificed to our need for activity. Perhaps
because activity itself is applauded and affirmed in our culture, and
is so addictive.

As long as we are frantic we needn't ask whether our lives matter.
Nor will we have a moment to ask how we are spending time and
"spending" our lives. Quietly checking what our attitudes are
around time can be challenging, even confronting. It may involve
giving up or redefining what we call important. It may involve
listening more attentively to what we tell ourselves about time:
who and what deserve our time, and what doesn't.

It takes courage as well as time to discover how time is using
us. Or how we could be using time. But we owe ourselves that. At
least that.

Open to Beauty

᯽

In our dizzyingly visual society much of what passes for beauty is barely skin deep. Yet, for all that, the need to be in the presence of beauty is strong in almost everyone. So is our need to create beauty, even in the most modest and unremarkable ways. Our spirits lift in the presence of beauty; they sink in its absence.

But acknowledging how crucial beauty is to our souls and emotions doesn't in itself solve the question of what beauty is, nor the extent to which our self-confidence and inner serenity and balance may depend upon it. Nor how our eyes (and ears) and therefore judgments are socially and culturally conditioned.

I was at a gathering recently where there was much earnest talk about the increasingly narrow equation of beauty with youth. The irony here is that young adults are seldom convinced of their own beauty or get much pleasure from it. They may struggle to handle the power that comes with good looks, or the eagerness of others to exploit them. They may fear the envy of their peers or how superficially other people judge and respond to them. Then, as they age, they may dread the loss of their looks—even when being beautiful has been fraught.

We speak so carelessly of someone losing their looks by early middle age (or of our own loss of looks) but in doing this we are buying into an extremely limited view of what "good looks" are, and of what beauty is.

I surely can't be alone in finding older people increasingly attractive. I can see how beautiful youth often is, sometimes especially in those who don't match contemporary stereotypes. I deeply appreciate the beauty of my adult children and their friends. For all that, I certainly don't feel that beauty stops there, nor in the generations older than my own. In fact, as my appreciation of much older people increases I wonder how much of this belated admiration is biological rather than ideological or socially conditioned.

Are we internally primed to value the different beauty of older age as we age ourselves? Whatever its genesis, this broadening focus certainly helps me to see older generations through increasingly rosy glasses, while also seeing the poignancy and charm of fleeting youthful beauty.

NATURE IN MOST of its many moods is an unfailing source of awe as well as beauty. Trees can provide as much depth and delight of "view" as water can. A glimpse of the night sky, or a cityscape, an unexpectedly enlarged vista as we turn a corner: all of this can lift our spirits and connect us more joyfully to the earth.

Music gives us moments of unparalleled, moving beauty (I am listening to Arvo Pärt's sublime "Spiegel im Spiegel" as I write this). Music also brings to life powerful associations. In this case, I am remembering that I first heard this music at a meditation class I regularly attended for some years. I feel the tenderness and sociability of that time as well as the tenderness in this music and especially in the yearning expressed by the cellist.

For me there is so much ecstasy as well as beauty in the vision-ary poetry that I love and read most often, and occasionally and unfashionably learn by heart. A friend's hug can bring beauty to life. So do the enchanting smiles of my little granddaughter. So do new and old prayers of trust or consolation.

As someone who is comfortable with a variety of religious and spiritual traditions, I love the beauty of sacred rituals, when time slows or ceases to matter. I love to pray and meditate in company, as much as I do alone. I love the "parting of the veils" when beauty or yearning or sometimes pain shows me that the worlds of here and beyond are one.

But perhaps I cherish most the expression of beauty and care in all its most intimate and domestic forms: the trouble someone takes to arrange brightly colored vegetables on a platter before bringing it to the table; the preparations we make for a simple afternoon tea; candles in the courtyard on a hot summer's night; homegrown and freshly picked flowers; a favorite painting come to life in a new spot; children's art honored in splendid rococo frames; a collage of family photos in a hallway; carefully chosen cushions, throws and lamps bringing instant change to a familiar sitting room; bright orange and gold on a favorite shawl; white in all its many shades; a single flower stem in a simple vase against a bare wall.

WE NEED such moments on a daily basis. Creating or simply attending to small and great experiences of beauty settles us. It connects us to our own inner sense of the "deepest things." It adds a much-needed depth to our lives that can convince us that it is not just life that matters, but our own unique gift of life playing its small part in the vastness we call "inner" and "outer."

A few days after I wrote those words I went with friends to an intimate dress rehearsal of a series of new dances being prepared by a leading contemporary dance company. The exquisite choreography allowed most of the dancers a few individual moments in the spotlight yet what was most exhilarating, and unexpectedly touching, was how poignant and affecting the truly ensemble moments were. In those moments, the individuality of the dancers largely faded, yet their willingness to be part of and contribute to the larger whole emerged as something specifically courageous, tender and beautiful. What also struck me was how varied the company members were, and how lovely this was to observe at close quarters. Of course they shared youth, vitality and a rare talent, but some were tiny, others tall; some obviously strong, some almost dangerously fragile; some danced with easy joy, others with a dramatic, coiled intensity, and those variations, too, added texture to the enchanting whole.

BEAUTY OF CHARACTER is also priceless and too often overlooked. During my Catholic girlhood, long ago, it was commonplace to call someone "beautiful" if they were generous, patient, bighearted or kind. I loved the phrase then and I love it now.

Someone who cultivates and expresses those qualities is truly beautiful. And becomes increasingly so. We still instinctively respond to the beauty of those characteristics and warm to the people who have them. What I find most glorious is that they are characteristics that grow more beautiful still with practice. And with age.

A Weight Off Your Mind

❀

I am no weight-loss expert. But perhaps most people who write diet books or promote diet products are not especially expert either. They may be able to tell you which foods to cut out or down. Or urge more exercise. But what they can't do is help you keep weight off in a sustained way.

Almost three out of four Americans are overweight or obese. The statistics are probably not so different in most other Western countries. When I'm out and about I see far more heavily overweight people than even a decade ago. I also see parades of magazine covers shrieking about which celebrity has lost a few miserable ounces or gained them. Very often people's sense of self or self-respect appears to be determined by their weight. There is much that's obscene about this. Yet for all this obsessive focus on food and body image (and surely in part because of it), people constantly fail at dieting.

The reasons aren't hard to find. Most diets are restrictive, boring and implicitly punitive. They remind you constantly of what you can't have. And of what you should not have had or done in the past. They also keep your attention on your food and your body in unhelpful ways. What's more, because diets focus so drearily and intensely on what goes into your mouth, they cannot pay attention to the far more crucial questions of what's happening in your mind and feelings when you think about food or long for it.

I want to say something provocative: that we will change our eating habits only when we think about food positively rather than punitively and when we think about our need for food with far greater love and appreciation than is usual.

When it comes to food and especially our attitudes toward it, *thoughts matter far more than our stomachs*. People who consistently eat too much are almost always using food to soothe emotional as well as physical hungers. Those hungers are real. They can feel as vast as a crater. But unless we can think about food and ourselves with far greater acceptance, trust and kindness, food will rarely fill us up.

It makes a real difference to think about what you can have, rather than what you can't; what would be delicious and delightful, rather than what is forbidden. It also makes a real difference to make your positive, rewarding choices out of love, not guilt.

Eat the very best food you can afford

If we feel guilty about food as well as our attitudes toward it, we often stuff ourselves with fast food or even other people's leftovers. It's as though we must acknowledge for the shortest possible time that we are indeed hungry. Deciding what food you most want already makes you more discerning. Eating the freshest, best quality food slowly enough to get pleasure from it, you will find that smaller portions and proportions take care of themselves.

Choose with love

From earliest childhood, most of us enjoy the comfort and pleasure that food gives. Make this less complicated by paying more attention to taste, texture, color and quality. Pleasure depends on taste, not volume. *Tasting* the food, eating slowly, savoring it, can become a positive part of your new eating rituals. Know that the comfort food can give is real—but limited. Develop other ways, too, to comfort, soothe and uplift yourself.

Know that some of your eating habits are simply habits

They can be changed. If you think you *have to* eat vast quantities of bread, pasta, potatoes, fatty foods or sweets, try telling yourself that you will now choose your foods on a meal-by-meal basis, rather than feeling driven or compelled by unhelpful patterns.

Eat slowly

When it comes to food, speed matters. You may be thinking about food almost constantly yet eat in a rush or a daze. ("What *was* that on my plate?") Eat at half your usual pace. Chew slowly. Put your cutlery down between bites. Even when you eat alone, sit at the table and rediscover ritual as well as pleasure.

Stop eating as soon as you are full

While discovering what "full" feels like, visualize your stomach as the size of a fist. (Lots of fresh vegetables fit into a fist.) Stopping may mean leaving food on your plate. Throw it in the bin. Don't *be* the bin.

Eat lots of protein as well as vegetables

Eating small amounts of protein frequently has made the biggest difference to my eating habits and weight. Sometimes I eat protein four to five times in a day, in small amounts. This reduces cravings and it cuts out the drive to overeat because you've become too hungry. Combine your protein with vegetables, fruit, unprocessed grains for essential glucose.

Eat when you are hungry

(But don't shop when you are hungry.) Don't eat because everyone else is eating or the clock says it's a mealtime. Don't eat because you are frustrated or bored. If you aren't hungry, don't eat. Check first to see if you are thirsty. Sometimes water is perfect. If you are "never hungry," that's a clear sign you are missing some vital signals from your body. It may help to eat frequent small meals of tasty, nutritious food. Let the food itself wake up your senses.

Learn to distinguish between being hungry for food and being emotionally hungry

Ask yourself, "What am I needing right now?" When you are hungry for the "worst" foods it is often because you are anxious, bored or lonely. None of those feelings is comfortable but food doesn't fix them. (If food could fix them that would have happened long ago!) *Noticing* what's going on gives you choice. Be aware, too, how often overeating is an immediate reflex. Let the moment pass and the craving with it.

Learn to soothe yourself

The capacity to talk yourself "up" rather than "down" will improve every aspect of your life. It will also affect what and how you eat. Focus on your strengths. Discover new ways of living with greater vitality. Let your mind settle using a soothing phrase or with a brief, easy focus on slow breathing.

Enough pleasure on your plate?

Often people overeat, or eat the foods that give them an instant high rather than nourishing them, when there is too little joy, interest or pleasure in their lives. Take some time to think about people and situations that stimulate, appreciate and engage you—and seek out those people and situations far more actively. Consider, too, how delightful it is to be so busy that you have to feel seriously hungry before you notice it, and start eating. Can you have more of that kind of intense activity? How? Where? Allow your life to be full, even when it means taking new risks or developing quite new appetites.

Take many steps

Slim people walk at least six thousand steps a day on average; overweight people walk on average only about two thousands steps less. Those two thousand additional steps count. Look for every opportunity to keep your body moving.

Love your life and body

When you are not sure what this means, simply ask—as you make a choice or decision—"Is this kind? Is this uplifting? Is this nourishing to my spirit as well as my body?" Let your immediate responses be your guide.

Your Own Best Expert

✼

In a time of trouble or at a crossroads moment, your experiences—and what you've learned from them—could be the most valuable asset you have. What's more, as long as your memory and sense of self are intact, they are yours for life.

Impossible to condense on your résumé, impossible to avoid when it comes to the lines on your face, this is the "all" of it all: the disastrous, the trivial, the heavenly and hellish. Better yet, the insights that come from your experiences can and will help you as nothing else can, *especially when things are not going well.*

After all, who knows you better than you do? Who's been there at every turn, if not you? Who else can convince you—repeatedly in tough times—that you have gotten through difficult situations before and you will again? Who can best persuade you that you can go on, that life is good—even when all seems most confusing or tragic?

Good and bad: those potent insights should never be wasted.

SOMETIMES IT TAKES a huge jolt for us to remember what we have *already* learned and *already* know. So many of us take the opposite tack when we are in a panic. We run around asking other people what they think we should do. And we take it for granted that their insights, even their "solutions," will be far more valuable than our own. This assumes that other people are wiser than you are. Or that they know far more about you and your situation than you do. The latter, at least, is almost never true.

Looking in from the outside, other people may indeed see things you don't. They may see patterns of behavior or reactions you are hiding from yourself. They might have heard your favorite stories a hundred times and can perceive just where you are stuck. Nevertheless, on the "how this happened" and "what to do next" questions, *you are your own best expert*. Or you can be.

IN THE FACE of a crisis, finding someone else to blame is extremely tempting. So is rushing blindly into a new adventure, getting drunk or overworking, or having an affair. Any of these will save you from quiet reflection. But these behaviors can also take you into the kind of scenario where you have been married five times and are still wondering why your luck with partners is so bad; where you have lost a dozen jobs and still believe that every boss is picking on you; where you are losing your temper on a daily basis while telling yourself that other people are the cause and trigger and that it's they, rather than you, who should "get over it."

Giving your own experiences little or no value, and ignoring the patterns in your choices and behavior, adds to that illusion of powerlessness. So does a constant search for someone else to blame or save you. Things do happen to us *and* we play our part.

We can't change what has happened. But we can certainly take charge of our part.

Allowing yourself to review your experiences is always enlightening. It may also be surprising. Patterns will emerge. Insights will come from that. You may well recall behavior that causes you shame. But even seeing that clearly, and *noticing what you can change*, is essential to that greater sense of self-determination that will be your most significant asset and driver as you move ahead.

THINKING ABOUT your past experiences—and their commonalities—you will also discover what got you through, what strengths you called upon, what insights you had and could have again. Perhaps the constancy of friends saved you. Maybe in the midst of your own distress you were nevertheless able to reach out and help someone else. Perhaps in those dark or tough moments of the past, you were able to pray or ask someone unexpected to support you. Maybe there were times when you removed yourself in due course from what could have been a worse situation.

Looking back, you might also see and understand that some of your old strategies clearly were *not* helpful. (Getting drunk again with your most embittered pal . . . Binge eating . . . Withdrawing from the friends who care most.) You might let the force of this insight support you to try out something more appropriate to this moment in your life, something that will strengthen you and take you forward.

This might include talking honestly and without self-pity to someone with a genuinely positive view of life. It might include finding a greater ability to compromise than you have previously shown. Or a new willingness to listen. It might mean finding the humility at last to accept someone else's point of view. Or seeing yourself as capable of greater self-control. It could include therapy or counseling if that would be helpful. Or taking charge of how much sleep and healthy food you are getting. It will certainly mean making good a resolve to see the bigger picture, no matter how down and hopeless you feel, plus seeking out and enjoying good company and *being* better company for yourself and others.

To BENEFIT FROM your own history, you don't need a new situation to be exactly like anything you have been through before. The nature of your current crisis is much less crucial than discovering and *valuing* what you have already survived, *valuing* freshly what your life has already taught you, and *valuing* yourself along with it.

Make Up Your Own Mind

⁂

Make up your mind" is a phrase rarely used without some undercurrent of frustration. It is likely to be thrown at us when we can't seem to act decisively. Or when we can't choose instantly between competing possibilities. We might use it ourselves if we know what we want and someone else seems to be dithering. It's a phrase that sends a strong message of criticism—as though instant decision-making was itself a virtue, regardless of the seriousness of the situation.

But surely only some decisions can and perhaps should be made quickly. If we are deciding between the white jeans or the black, between taking the kids to the park or the pool, between writing a report now or later, then it relieves our own stress as well as everyone else's to decide quickly. I have a friend who likes to say, "When neither choice is 'wrong,' go for the one that's simplest or most uplifting."

In our rushed, complex lives, that rule could help us more often than we may think. Following it, we could keep many everyday decisions fuss-free. And if you find it hard to distinguish a big decision from a small one, ask yourself if you are likely to remember it a week from now. Only something that has long-term consequences is worth fretting about. And, even then, fretting is rarely helpful.

IN LIVES as privileged as most of ours are, "choice" has real meaning. We can make up our minds about our most fundamental decisions including our lifestyle, values, relationships, beliefs and goals. We can't determine everything that happens to us, but we can certainly decide how we are going to respond. And we can learn from our mistakes when our strategies take us in the wrong direction. (When it comes to making choices, "older and wiser" may have some real currency!)

Making up our minds, we can evaluate the notion of choice itself and what choice means to us individually. We soon learn that we make choices within a highly charged cultural context. Seeing that, we can begin more confidently to take charge of what comes into our minds and lives and what most obviously influences us.

GIVING minimal energy to the minor choices frees us up for the choices that will and do matter. Making up our own minds is a precious freedom. It means we are not letting circumstances or other people run our lives for us. Self-responsibility triumphs here. So does insight. Taking charge of our choices, we discover what our priorities are. And what we most cherish.

Making up our minds then becomes something bigger than deciding between this career or that, making a new start in a relationship or walking away, speaking up in a difficult situation or remaining silent.

On the big issues, and especially when the consequences affect other people, making up our minds is not always achieved instantly. Sometimes it takes weeks of reflection. And if what we face is a crossroads moment, when what we choose will truly matter, I believe we owe it to ourselves to reflect deeply, even when this takes time as well as patience.

TRUSTING YOU CAN make small decisions with a light heart, and bigger ones more thoughtfully, builds your self-confidence immeasurably. Better still, your confidence isn't dependent on making the right decisions every time. Every thoughtful person I know has made a plentiful share of unwise choices. I certainly have. But they (and I) have moved on by facing and learning from them: neither wallowing in self-pity nor blaming other people or life's unfairness. It's those twin capacities of self-responsibility and self-awareness that best help us to know our own minds. And that best teach us how and when to make them up wisely.

The Almost Perfect Ego

Sigmund Freud is no longer a giant on the cultural landscape. And he's never been the giant for me that some other psychological innovators have, including Carl Jung, Viktor Frankl and Roberto Assagioli. Nonetheless, some of Freud's concepts do remain useful as reference points in our self-understanding. Many people draw freely on his insights about the unconscious and conscious realms of the mind, for example, and particularly on his identification of the ego as a key aspect of the human psyche, a kind of interface between our inner and outer worlds.

No one, of course, has ever actually seen or measured an ego (although most of us have felt its effects). We are talking about a concept, not a fact. Yet somehow we instinctively know what we have come to call the ego as something that is both palpable and powerful.

In everyday life, we often speak about ego in terms of "too much" or, less often, "too little." Too much ego, or being noticeably egotistical, has come to mean that someone has an inflated sense of their own importance. They may put themselves forward too eagerly. They may be immensely competitive, vying constantly with others around even trivial matters. Often they find it hard to take other people's lives or points of view seriously. They may bring every conversation back to their own experiences. They may be insatiable for attention, praise or success—yet rarely get enough.

This means that while being around a person who appears to be ego-driven is sometimes exciting, especially if they are creative and energetic, it's not likely to be comfortable. And because someone with an inflated ego needs and demands so much attention, it's unlikely to be mutually rewarding in the longer run.

THE EGO IS only part of a much bigger and incomplete theory of the human psyche. Freud attempted to describe humankind's highly complex psychology by suggesting that we each have an id, driven by instincts and self-focused appetites; a super-ego, ideally driving a conscience that is reliable and sensitive, but (on bad days) sometimes highly critical, intolerant and moralizing; and also an ego, which Freud himself called *das Ich* (the "I").

Most of us will grow in self-confidence and in our confidence to relate well to other people once our ego is in check: when it's neither too big nor too small. Our best chance to achieve this comes from paying rather less attention to ourselves (neither inflated nor anxious) and a good deal more to how we are affecting those around us.

The highly self-focused or egotistical person doesn't have much concern for other people, except when they are meeting their needs. They may be nakedly ambitious, but this shouldn't be confused with a strong ego. Even less should it be confused with a stable sense of self.

When someone is routinely demanding, controlling and never wrong—or is quiet and timid but chronically self-involved—this often masks considerable anxiety and inner agitation: signs of a "weak" ego and insecure sense of self. The lucky person whose ego is in check doesn't have to dominate every situation they are in or demand constant applause. They can make mistakes without blaming someone else, and they can enjoy and take an interest in other people's achievements without envying them. Most crucially, they don't depend on putting others down in order to feel "up."

How WE THINK about and judge ego has become as much a cultural phenomenon as it is a psychological one. Even a casual reading of contemporary media will reveal highly ambiguous attitudes about the degree of self-involvement it takes to achieve unusual success. Increasingly we drive our children and ourselves hard. We worship what success seems to promise. Yet both resentment and schadenfreude thrive in twenty-first-century life, driving the relish we display when someone famous or successful is brought down publicly.

This doesn't reflect well on us individually. It is also a sad comment on our collective psyche, because the more we feel entitled to mock or crush other people, the more fragile our own inner confidence and ego are shown to be.

In one of the loveliest and most basic of human paradoxes, we develop a healthy ego, self-awareness and self-mastery not through long hours spent at the mirror, or by driving our own agenda as though nothing else matters, but through relationships with other people and particularly through the unique challenges of intimacy.

For intimacy to succeed, we have to learn to compromise and cooperate. This helps us to understand that our agenda can't always prevail and that failing to get our own way won't kill us. We function best and we feel best once we have woken up to the reality that we are not the center of the universe and that our happiness will almost certainly depend on how well we connect with others. When one person has to control another, put another down, or transgress their boundaries and sense of self, there is no intimacy.

FREUD ALSO famously pointed out that human beings need work as well as love. Beyond the essential paycheck, work gives us purpose and a much-needed external shape to our days. But how we feel about our work, what satisfaction we get from it and whether we are inclined to be a thoughtful colleague or the office bully also depends on our ego strength.

A strong ego and a reliable sense of self makes life not just bearable but sometimes sublime. In some spiritual circles, there is open distaste for the ego as something to transcend. But that is to misunderstand it. We need *das Ich* to live securely in the world. And we also need it to comprehend that "the world" extends way beyond our individual selves.

Surviving the Global Stress Crisis

✺

No one seems to know if we have fully recovered from the global financial crisis or are hurtling toward another round. Economic issues remain perennially concerning. Wars, too, continue to be waged in our "peaceful" world. Cataclysmic natural disasters occur near and far from home. Significant numbers of the world's people are in need of shelter and safety. And I suspect that our collective peace of mind is also, as always, in need of attention.

INDIVIDUALS' STRESS LEVELS are highly sensitive to social conditions. As peace of mind plummets, along with self-confidence and trust in one another, stress levels rise. This doesn't affect emotional health and well-being only. It impinges on every aspect of our personal and collective lives and markedly affects whether we treat one another harshly or kindly.

Many people will insist that they are coping fine with whatever is thrown at them. Because people are often ashamed when they are barely coping, they may seem insulted if you inquire after their emotional health. They may, nevertheless, report a spate of physical symptoms. These can be as varied as chronic headaches, asthma,

digestive problems, under- or over-eating, excessive drinking, a sore
back, constant colds or flu, a general feeling of malaise, loss of
libido, breathlessness or a racing heart, high blood pressure and,
of course, sleeplessness.

Those familiar physical symptoms not only reflect emotional
stress, they add to it. If you are constantly unwell, chronically tired,
unfit or hungover it becomes difficult to make considered decisions
and monitor what's best for you at work or at home. To deal with
and *enjoy* contemporary life, you need to be in good shape both
inside and out. When you are not, even small additional setbacks or
burdens can become intolerable.

IT'S EASY TO FORGET you can also feel stressed when you are
*under*stimulated. Feeling useless, seeing yourself as disconnected
from any real social purpose, not stretching the mind in any new or
fresh way, caring little about anyone's welfare but your own: these
are all common experiences that are highly stressful. Fortunately,
they are also experiences that you can transform. Even when paid
work is no longer available, for example, it is possible to volunteer.
Even (and especially) when leaving the house seems too much, you
can and must, regardless of whether you "feel like it." As you take
action your feelings will change, not least because they no longer
rule you.

YET MORE OF US will feel highly stressed when it seems that life
itself is asking too much of us; when we can't meet the demands in
our lives or can't meet them in time or at the levels of productivity
or accuracy that are required of us. We will feel stressed when we

are exhausted, as new parents inevitably are, or when we are caring for other people and there is no respite in the foreseeable future. In this age of massive personal debt, many of us will feel immensely stressed when we are under financial pressure. And when our health is under siege, when we have a serious diagnosis of a physical or mental illness, that's also hugely stressful. It is stressful for us and for everyone who loves us.

STRESS PRODUCES anxiety—and worsens it. For many people, this results in worrying even more than usual and with ever less sense of resolution or purpose. As our self-confidence topples, this may mean high levels of agitation, irritability, frustration and intolerance of other people or their attempts to help.

Those symptoms of stress make difficult situations worse. Ironically, this is good to know because often the stress symptoms can be lessened even while the difficult situation continues.

Panic, anxiety or depression, self-pity or feelings of helplessness, as well as manic responses, intensify stress. This is because they limit people's cognitive as well as emotional responses. They make it harder to take in new information, listen well or think creatively or strategically. The anxious person may become quite stuck in their thinking, withdrawn, or quick to jump to gloomy conclusions. None of that helps the sufferer or makes life any easier for those around them.

TELLING OURSELVES that we have no power to effect change worsens stress and is rarely true. Even in the most testing circumstances we retain some choice about how we will *describe* a situation to ourselves, how we will *claim* or marshal our resources, how we will *ask for and receive help*, and whether we are willing to *nurture* some sense of hope or meaning.

The desire to withdraw into the cave of their own fears is strong in many people when their stress levels are high. Yet, unsurprisingly, this is a time when help is often needed, not least to see the situation with greater clarity.

Learning to monitor and manage stress is a quintessential twenty-first-century task. We have to discover how to subdue our own inner agitation and not add to the agitation all around us.

It's far too easy to get into a frame of mind where you believe that time or life or your goals are running you, rather than trusting yourself to take charge of your life as you can and should. Discovering that you can audit your choices and respond more assertively or creatively to stressful situations can be life changing. Often that's what skillful coaching or counseling will help you to achieve. The right book at the right time can also be a tremendous ally.

I like a straightforward book like *Stop Thinking, Start Living* by Richard Carlson. My own practical book, *Choosing Happiness*, offers many strategies. Timothy Sharp's *Happiness Handbook* is also immediately helpful, while Martin Seligman's *Learned Optimism* is also sound and helpful. What each of these books can do is help you *to tell yourself a more positive story* about who you are and what you are capable of doing and being. This is significant. When we are in a panic, or feeling as though we are drowning in responsibilities or demands— or that life has deserted us—we need to find a way forward that rebuilds our self-confidence, reminds us of our strengths, and lets us see our situation through more self-affirming, hopeful eyes.

When anyone is suffering from symptoms of stress I also warmly recommend taking up journal writing. It can be almost magically helpful to discover how to empty your thoughts onto the welcoming pages of a journal. In fact, as someone who has been a skilled worrier since earliest childhood, I long ago discovered that problem solving or pouring out your thoughts in the pages of a journal is far more helpful than lying awake at 3 a.m. and worrying your way toward dawn.

STRESS IS EVERYWHERE in our world. That doesn't make unendurable levels of it normal or necessary. Aware that your stress levels are rising, that your blood pressure is a worry or that you feel far more irritable or low than usual, you can do something about it—for the sake of others as much as yourself.

Taking that first step may be at least as demanding as any of the heroic physical challenges we so admire. What's more, it involves some of the same steps: defining your priorities, determining what action is needed, dealing with one step at a time, and ruthlessly limiting what is undermining or unimportant.

Making those changes will always give you at least some sense of taking charge and moving forward, almost regardless of whatever dire or challenging external circumstances would otherwise hold you back.

Check Your Assumptions
(They May Be Wrong)

To a great extent our self-confidence is determined by the way we think. And perhaps especially by how we think about what others are thinking, especially when it concerns us. Some of us are ludicrously confident that we can read other people's minds. And never more so than when it comes to criticisms or put-downs ("You think that I'm . . . ," "I know he doesn't think that I can . . . ," "You always . . . ," "You never . . .").

Few of us, though, are skilled mind readers. And in bad times our accuracy levels will plummet. Even in good times, we can only imagine what others are thinking (although we can certainly take note of their responses and behaviors). In fact, we can take it as a given that whenever we are feeling out of sorts or anxious, whatever we assume others are thinking will almost certainly be wrong.

What happens in those situations, and particularly when emotions are heightened, is that we project our own worst fears onto other people. We attribute our own thoughts to them ("She thinks I am a neglectful father. . . ."). Those other people's judgments do indeed seem convincing, but that's *because they were actually born and took life in our own minds.*

No surprise then that we so often react to our own assumptions, or defend ourselves against these terrifying paper tigers, causing chaos and confirming our worst fears as we do so.

- We feel fat—and "know" other people are judging us for it.
- We feel insecure or uncertain—and assume we "look stupid" in other people's eyes.
- We feel self-loathing—and accuse others of putting us down or letting us down.
- We are overwhelmed by self-pity—and discount and demean other people, accusing them of all the things we most fear or dislike in ourselves.
- We know that our behavior is dishonest—and accuse others of hypocrisy or lying.
- We find a small fault in someone else and behave as though World War Three is about to begin. Then we blame the other person for causing the outburst by failing to anticipate our every want.

It's all too easy to attribute to other people the darkest thoughts that are in our own minds. This can lead to catastrophic misunderstandings, defensive and attacking behaviors and often, in time, to a relationship breakdown.

TAKE IT AS A GIVEN that when you fear (or believe you can predict) what other people are thinking about you, *you are more likely to be wrong than right.*

They are almost certainly judging you far less harshly than you are judging yourself. Chances are, actually, that they are not thinking about you at all. And if their thoughts are indeed attacking or bleak? That says more about their insecurities than yours.

Unless you are living in an abusive relationship, your worst attacker will almost always be yourself. (If you are living in a verbally abusive relationship it is crucial that you get professional help. Being told that you are a horrible or worthless person is frightening and morally and emotionally bankrupting. It is always a serious, inexcusable breach of trust.)

It also helps to know that when we are attacking others (or fearing that they are thinking badly of us), this reveals in us a deep insecurity and lack of self-worth. It is a problem of self-acceptance and self-confidence. It is not a problem caused by or even exacerbated by the other person.

Anyone who feels inwardly secure will attribute at least reasonably positive thoughts to other people. And, crucially, they will not attack because they feel under attack from within. They will also feel unafraid to check out their fears ("Did you think I was overreacting when I got so upset the other day with Joe?").

AND IF WE HAVE indeed done something wrong? And are worried with good reason about what others will think of us?

Be assured that anyone who is in good shape psychologically will see our behavior or choices as part of the bigger picture, not as a disaster and rarely as a tragedy. They won't see our mistakes as an insult to *them*. Making mistakes is part of life. Failing to anticipate someone's wishes is part of life. People doing and seeing things differently is part of life. As some would say, "Get over it!"

Life would be extremely small if we never tried things out, stumbled, fell and got up again. If we have done something wrong, apologies are in order. And a convincing determination not to make the same mistake again. If there is nothing wrong other than our own churning misery, we need to do something about it.

The crucial thing is to be *aware of what we are attributing to other people and what more properly belongs in our own mind and psyche—* which is where we can do something about it.

THESE SMALL SHIFTS in attention and awareness are fundamental to our personal integrity. They determine our self-confidence. They remind us, too, that while we can't control what other people think, we can certainly do something about our own thoughts.

Better still, we can learn to monitor, choose and "direct" our own interpretations in much more positive ways.

Think dark thoughts in the privacy of your own mind, stew on genuine or perceived hurts, attribute dark thoughts to the people around you (and behave accordingly), and *your inner and outer worlds will be bleak.*

By contrast, assume a positive attitude, develop tolerance of your own and others' inevitable complexity, and not only will it matter far less what other people think of you but you can trust that they will think about you warmly, kindly and with increasing appreciation. As vitally, you will think about them with a similar ease.

Could any change of mind be more worthwhile? Or more rewarding?

RELATIONSHIPS

✳

Don't Work at It!

Loving Well (and Well Loved)

Marriage Forecasts

How to Save Your Marriage!

Long Live Romance

Power Sharing

Housework, Sex and Power

Needs at Odds

Passion and Possession

All Grown Up

Perfect Lover, True Friend

Don't Work at It!

꙳

Two words long overdue for a divorce are "work" and "relationship." I would be rich if I had a cent for each time someone has said to me with utter sincerity, "We need to work harder on our relationship." Or, "Relationships take so much hard work."

Help!

Just think about all our associations with the word "work." Primary among them is that work is . . . well, *work*. It requires effort. It gobbles up much of your life. You are constantly judged for it. You can be dropped or demoted at any time. Your opinions are welcome only if they flatter or intrigue the people who are far more important than you are.

And then there's money. You get *paid* to work. And often that's work's biggest reward. But however much or little you get paid, work makes you tired. You need weekends and holidays to recover from it and to prepare for more of it. Work adds to your status or detracts from it. Either way, you worry about it. You may also worry about questions of meaning. Is the work you have chosen the best you can do? And "best" by what standards? Who are you there to please? Does it foster your social skills, your creativity and inner

well-being? Or are we back again to the pay envelope, the bills and
your need to survive?

Think, now, about relationships. Think about pleasure, interest,
companionship, vulnerability, encouragement, understanding, cooperation, security, support and trust. Think about happiness, gratitude and contentment. Think about someone regarding you as the
most important person in their world. Think about *love*.

WHEN A RELATIONSHIP is going downhill, or is causing more
heartache than healing, what it may well need is less *work* and far
more of all the good things. It may need more consideration. It will
certainly need more kindness. And far greater enthusiasm. It may
need more separateness and less anxiety about that. It may need
more togetherness and less tension with that.

People may need to remind themselves what there is to rejoice in
rather than complain or worry about.

IS THAT KIND of awareness *work*? Is it *work* to make sure you are
having supportive, engaging conversations, rather than the tedious
exchange of views and instructions that some couples accept as
inevitable? Is it *work* to banish criticism and find several things each
day that you can appreciate or laugh about out loud? Is it *work* to
hold your partner when they are exhausted or grieving or have been
up all night to finish a report or comfort a baby and promise them
that things will get better? Is it *work* to get dressed up to go out
together, even if it is only to a café for coffee or a local beauty spot?
Is it *work* to turn up the music and dance in the kitchen—especially
when all the chores are not yet done? Is it *work* to let go of the

delusion that your partner should be reading your mind and ful-filling your every unexpressed need? Is it *work* to bury ancient, terminally dull resentments and come with new vigor and thrill right into this present, irreplaceable moment?

MOST PEOPLE do best when they *work* at work and *relate* with interest, patience, curiosity and delight in their relationships.

It is that simple.

Loving Well
(and Well Loved)

꧁

We all know that what the world needs now is love sweet love (please sing along . . .)! But because it's so hard to talk about love, even while we need it as much as we do air and water, we remain somewhat unsure of what exactly it is, queasy about what we most want and uncertain about what we are giving and getting.

Our fear of sentimentality is so great that sometimes it seems easier to retreat into a defensive cynicism. It's also easy to see love as something private that only occasionally pushes its way into the public sphere. Yet the desire for love and respect is deep in the human spirit. It crosses cultures. It's existed throughout recorded time. And it's clear that the happiest people we are lucky enough to know are those who are most broadly and consistently loving.

My observation is that such people don't save their best selves for one or two people only. They may certainly have their intimate and most meaningful relationships, but they engage positively with *life* and use the power we all have to encourage and make other people feel appreciated, respected and special.

. . .

INTERESTINGLY (and unsurprisingly), the people who are broadly loving of other people, nature, the universe and the whole great mystery of life are also the people *least* likely to be anxiously demanding of those closest to them. And that makes sense.

If your vision of love is limited to just a few people, or to the "one and only," that makes you vulnerable. Vulnerability *is* the shadow of love; there's no avoiding it. The day we fall deeply in love with a life partner, the day our children are born, the day we meet the friend who will become a soul mate are all days on which knowledge of our vulnerability hits home.

Love is worth it. Love insists we bear it.

Love emerges from a sense of possibility as well as connection. It takes us forward, in addition to making the present moment sweeter. Anyone who seeks to control or possess another person in the name of love is confused about what love is. Fear and lack of self-trust are what makes people cling, control and complain. So how good it is to know that while love can and does make us more vulnerable, it need not make us more fearful.

From love we learn how to give of ourselves. Doing that, we discover what our strengths are. We also develop them. At the same time, we discover that we don't need to be perfect to love well. Nor do we need to be perfect to be well loved. We can accept other people's ordinary human failings (along with our own). We can focus on what is pleasing. We can speak up, affirm and grow our gratitude.

IT IS LOVE that teaches us that other people's lives matter and that the quality of our own lives will depend on how loving our everyday connections are. Love may take second place to work in too many of our lives, but it's the steadiness and depth of our relationships that will convince us how rich life is.

It's also love that invites us to open to difference. We can share interests and values with those we love while celebrating all the ways we are not the same. Love makes differences stimulating. Loving others—robustly and imperfectly—also lets us love and accept ourselves. This doesn't mean being narcissistic. In fact, living lovingly and enthusiastically is the best possible cure for anxious self-absorption. It saves us from requiring someone else to convince us that we are lovable. It opens our eyes as well as our hearts to the intricate, intimate reality of other people.

Marriage Forecasts

The guru of marriage, American academic and writer Dr. John Gottman, visited Australia a year or two ago. I had the good fortune to be speaking at the same conference ("Happiness and Its Causes," in Sydney). This gave me the chance to observe him up close, so I can say confidently that if white-haired, bright-eyed, gnomish, yarmulke-wearing psychologists were permitted several wives, thousands of women would be vying for a spot.

It is not, however, for his wit and brilliance only that Dr. Gottman stands out from the crowd but for his observations about committed intimacy—both gay and straight—and his confidence that he can pick which intimate relationships will flourish and which won't.

In the gospel according to Gottman, a crucial element that determines success or failure is conflict. Not its absence, as you might expect—some clash of needs is inevitable—but, rather, how it's dealt with. Does each partner have sufficient flexibility, goodwill and plain common sense to de-escalate times of conflict or difference? Or do they make conflict worse with defensive and often offensive counterattacks or hostile behaviors? In other words, when your partner is tense, upset or out of sorts, or has opinions or needs that fail to harmonize neatly with your own, how you deal with those moments will make a massive difference to the happy-ever-after outcome that most people still ardently want.

GOTTMAN has widely reported through his books and talks that he and his team of researchers have also explored how much positivity (interest, communication, affirmation, encouragement) is needed to maintain intimacy. And they have compared this with how much negativity (belittling, whining, ignoring, criticizing, blaming) each partner can tolerate.

Gottman puts his positivity/negativity figure at 5:1. In other words, for every mean, discouraging or critical thing you say, you must have made at least five positive statements if the relationship is not to suffer. In extrahealthy relationships the figure is more like 20:1. That is, for every unkind or undermining statement, there will have been at least twenty experiences of explicit appreciation.

What that adds up to is that in flourishing relationships it's still possible to say what you don't want or like, if you must, but the rule is to do it infrequently, with great caution, and certainly without attacking, whining or blaming. (Take it as a cardinal rule that if you ever hear yourself speak to your partner like a belligerent parent or a prison warden you are taking the road to ruin.)

FONDNESS AND ADMIRATION are key Gottman principles. And aren't they usually why people get together in the first place? Aren't they usually what people *revel* in and want more of?

In fact, those uplifting practices are so crucial that their presence or absence will be obvious in minutes when people get together to talk about their relationship. Hence Gottman's famed capacity to tell you whether to go home and enjoy the rest of your lives together, or go home and pack your bags.

IT'S EASY to enjoy Gottman's findings. Without the formidable resources of his Seattle-based Gottman Relationship Institute, I have taken a similar line in my own long-term research and writing on intimacy. Like him, I am confident that commitment, loyalty, kindness, encouragement and tolerance are not just ideals but are crucial to maintaining love. Gottman's research proves it, but I would go further than he does and say that in most relationships *explicit criticism should be banned*. (Complaints, yes, if you must. But only when offered with extreme caution and a rigorous absence of heat or self-righteousness.)

This sounds tough. But the stakes are high. Better yet, even when people have had a rocky start, they can still learn the skills needed to make someone else happy and to be much happier themselves, particularly when they have a clear picture of what they risk losing.

Our individual well-being is central here. Doing well in our relationships is essential to our happiness. This extends beyond our intimate relationships but is probably tested most in the relationships where we are least guarded and most vulnerable. When we can freely appreciate and validate the person we claim to love, we make ourselves as well as our partner feel hopeful and positive as well as happy. And we are far more likely to have the kind of relationship we want.

. . .

LOVE CANNOT SURVIVE when we are often angry with another person, when we are resentful, belittling or chronically unappreciative. It cannot survive if we are afraid of our partner, either, especially when they also expect us to share their life and bed.

Relationships are the place where most of us have our best chance to grow up. They are also where we can learn most about compromise, and the generosity and empathy that compromise needs. Gottman's research is fascinating here, too. He has found that intimate relationships benefit when men are willing to compromise in disputes rather than taking a hard line or confusing compromise with weakness. When a man is able to look at things from his partner's perspective, it validates his partner *and* it acknowledges the importance of their relationship.

This makes sense. What people argue about is often irrelevant. Far more powerful is the need to be understood and to feel that you are on the same side rather than on opposing sides.

For a relationship to thrive, mutuality is key. This means a keen sense that "we are in this together," with neither one triumphing over the other so that both lose out.

Forgiveness matters too. And so does humor.

How to Save Your Marriage!

❧

If your marriage or love relationship is worth saving—and many are!—these ideas may help. They can give you a renewed awareness of how possible it is to lift your partner's spirits—and your own—with consistent, trustworthy attitudes and acts of kindness and consideration.

A mutually rewarding relationship is the most significant investment you will ever make. Your thoughtfulness and appreciation will create an atmosphere of trust and affection where everyone can flourish. Such behavior makes you easy to love and delightful to be around. It enhances your self-respect. It lifts your confidence in yourself as a genuinely loving person.

1. Be gracious. Offer at least as much courtesy and interest to your partner as you would to your most valued friend.
2. Remember how thrilling it was when you met? When this fine person looked your way and kept looking? See your partner as a separate person, complex and never entirely known. Take nothing for granted.
3. Enjoy one another's company. Create a life together that's more than shared and separate tasks.

4. Difference, even conflict is not itself a "problem." Problems come when you can't resolve conflict and differences intelligently. Your own interests are best served when you recognize that each of you depends for your happiness on the kindness and thoughtfulness of the other.

5. Learn to read your partner's body language. Notice what makes your partner more relaxed, trusting, comfortable, happier. Do more of it.

6. Silence your complaints. (They are never worth it. And will seldom get you what you want.) Speak up constantly about what's positive. Have more of that.

7. If you have children, know that they will learn respect and love from the way you and your partner treat one another. Be the example your children deserve.

8. No woman finds a man sexually attractive if he demeans her, trivializes her, blames her for his misery, tries to control her time, money, friends or thinking, or has no time to share housework and child care.

9. No man finds a woman endearing if she nags, intrudes on his private thoughts, demands that he pay her constant attention, spies on him or ridicules his friends, his body or his emotional deficits.

10. Do things together outside as well as inside the house. There's no need to share everything. But do share some things.

11. Your bad moods or ancient miseries do not justify criticism, sarcasm or verbal abuse. Those behaviors are fatal for your relationship. If you are chronically angry, you will be hard or impossible to live with. Do something about it for all your sakes.

12. Outbursts or accusations describe you far more accurately than they will your partner. Take notice.

13. Monitor your intimacy "entitlements." Your flashes of resentment can be brutally revealing. Bring your expectations right up to date.

14. Be very clear that your partner is not your parent.

15. Listen. Listen to what your partner has to say. Listen to how you speak to and about your partner. Is it uplifting? Is it encouraging and appreciative? Is it kind?

16. Keep your relationship alive in the present moment. Being married or committed to each other is a promise, not an end point. Every day can offer new interest and delight.

17. Be interested and interesting. Bring home the best of yourself, not the shell. Turn off the television. Put down your iPad. Silence your phone. Talk.

18. Share the responsibility (and credit) for everything that affects your relationship: housework, study, children, income, friends and extended family. This doesn't mean that every task is divided fifty-fifty. It does mean seeing each other as true partners in the life you are jointly creating.

19. Value the ways in which your partner is different from you. If you want someone who will think, act and react just like you, remember that you could have married your mirror.

20. Even if you don't believe in God, thank God every day for your continuing relationship. Regard it as your most precious achievement. Act accordingly.

Alas, it's also probably true that some marriages are not worth saving. If you are unhappy more often than not, if you or your partner is routinely hostile or abusive (especially if no one else knows), if you are in physical danger, if your partner is unwilling to get professional help for an addiction, bad temper or infidelity, or if your partner is unkind or abusive to your children, your focus should be on how to end the relationship and move on toward a healthier life of greater integrity. That can also be an act of courage and kindness.

Long Live Romance

❊

We had a wedding in our family recently and the happiness and optimism that it generated make it easy to think more generally about romance and its magic. Perhaps our own lovely occasion also made me more than usually appreciative of a couple of romantic stories that I've heard lately.

The first had its genesis in a local supermarket, where a gentle, openhearted woman I have known for some years fell into small talk with an attractive man who was also waiting in the slow checkout line. In best rom-com fashion, they exchanged jokes about doing their mundane food shopping on a Saturday night before walking out together. A few more minutes' easy talk outside the supermarket led to a coffee. A coffee led to a dinner. A dinner led within a year to their marriage.

This story is particularly lovely because these are two people well past the age where "going out on a Saturday night" is code for "meeting someone and hoping this time it will be special." The woman, she assured me, was ready for a change in her single existence. But it's hard to believe either of them would have expected anything other than groceries from this most innocent excursion.

.   .   .

THE OTHER ACCOUNT was one I heard at a formal dinner. About
ten of us were gathered around a table and as the young woman told
her story everyone was brought almost to tears by the beauty and
enchantment of what she was describing.

Kara is a delightful Anglo-Australian woman in her thirties. At
the time we all met, she had been married to her first-generation
Lebanese-Australian husband for only a matter of weeks, but her
preparations for the wedding had taken many months of thoughtful
planning.

Kara's husband has a few relatives in Sydney but most of his
family still live in Lebanon and had made the journey to Australia
just for their wedding. The culture of the wedding was largely
Arabic, and Kara described with great zest how she had trained
for months so that when the bridal party arrived at the island
where they were to hold their reception, she could literally dance
her way forward with the grace and boldness of a traditional dancer.

This she did, as drums played, guests clapped and called and as
her new husband clapped and danced alongside her. When they
reached the hall where the gala reception was to be held, Kara, her
husband and his parents were hoisted onto the shoulders of guests
and danced joyously around the room.

"My gorgeous Arabic wedding" was how she described it, but
the festivities didn't end there. When it came time for the speeches,
Kara stood and read in Arabic an entire speech that she had prepared and transliterated. Better than that, she had chosen someone
her husband had casually mentioned as having a beautiful accent to
coach her and help her prepare a speech in a language she so far
barely understands.

"As I was reading it I looked up," she told us, "a bit afraid that people might be laughing at my pronunciation, only to see that most people were crying with pleasure, including my husband."

Not only did Kara make her speech in Arabic, she also used cultural references to assure her new family how proud she was now to be one of them. Surely she could not have given her husband's family, and particularly her husband, a more exquisite gift or a more creative expression of her love.

ROMANCE TAKES US way beyond the ordinary and transforms it. Even witnessing other people's love lifts our spirits. Whether it is your partner, friend or loved ones, idealization is always part of this story. But so too are the priceless gifts of wonder and gratitude. Well beyond the first flush of love, unstinting appreciation and gratitude can sustain this gift indefinitely.

Men need romance as much as women, if sometimes differently. Anyone willing to nurture its enchantments is likely to be exceptionally happy. And also blessed.

Power Sharing

Intimate relationships, like close friendships, thrive when the people involved are openly and honestly committed to power sharing. Those same relationships will suffer or collapse when either person acts like a dictator—however benevolent they may be.

THE WAY POWER is exercised in our most intimate relationship will reflect with surprising accuracy how people feel about themselves. Those who feel generally good about themselves won't need to be constantly right. Nor will they need to get their own way every time. They can tolerate their own inconsistencies and complexities. They can tolerate the same surprises in other people.

When one person lays down the law and the other person "puts up with it," the outlook for both is bleak. Danger signs include throwing tantrums or punishing your partner, parent or friend when your agenda comes second. It also includes chronic helplessness or self-pity, putting the other person down so you can feel "up," and finding someone else to blame for your own behavior. Or, when things go wrong, refusing to listen or talk. It also includes making unchecked assumptions about what the other person should be doing, thinking or feeling. Oh, and using hot and cold behaviors as a means of control.

POWER CAN'T BE SHARED when either person sees the other as belonging to them. (We "own" clothes, books, furniture, houses and cars; *never* our partner or our children.) Power also can't be shared when people forget that their partner is a distinct, *separate* human being, however loved. Marriage is not a synonym for merging. Or, rather, two people who are committed to one another may merge their interests but not their sense of self: at least, not without unsustainable costs.

Power sharing depends upon an unconditional respect for boundaries, differences—and one another. And respect depends upon honest, fearless, *loving* communication. That often means more listening than talking. Listening to yourself, also, observing the effect as well as the content of what you are saying, and never silencing someone else with your barrage of words.

It certainly means thinking cooperatively ("What will benefit us both?") rather than reacting defensively. It means sharing problems and taking responsibility for them cooperatively.

Getting a little distance from a problem, "owning" it jointly, and solving it together can reap terrific results. Not only do you avoid blame and resentment, you will grow closer.

A more generous approach to power sharing, and a conscious sharing of blame, responsibility and especially credit, may seem to take more attention and time than most people believe they have. The rewards, though, are infinite. It brings kindness to life. It brings home (literally and symbolically) the impact of your choices. It lets you see your partner or friend as a distinct individual and not just someone who exists only in relation to you.

WOMEN CAN ABUSE POWER in intimate relationships as brutally as men, although class, money and gender expectations if unexamined will certainly play their part. The power to hurt is often exercised unconsciously as well as consciously. Some of the most unsettled and unsettling people I have worked with in therapy or other groups, or known in my private life, were least willing to acknowledge how much power they wield. Passive aggression is no more acceptable than any other form of violence. In any of its forms (withholding, bribing, manipulating, punishing with silence, refusing kindness or praise or ordinary courtesy), this is a hurtful, corrosive misuse of power, as is sustained helplessness.

THINKING ABOUT POWER, questioning your assumptions about who should be doing what and why, and talking openly and honestly about when you feel most challenged is a fine way to set up a more equitable and much more satisfying relationship between two grown-up people. How adults share power will radically affect their children's socialization. It will also determine whether they are fun to be with as a couple or to be avoided whenever possible. Perhaps most crucially, such discussions—and the experimentation those discussions are likely to provoke—are key to a greater self-awareness within each person. The relationship can only benefit.

Housework, Sex and Power

Complaints about housework and sex are painfully common in many households. That isn't news. Nor is it news that often what drives these clashes is a struggle around power. Or, perhaps more accurately, it is a struggle around appreciation: the power each partner has to affirm the other one—or to withhold this.

At a function recently I witnessed a couple—early forties, married about ten years—falling into a loud, quite abusive argument about housework. It was clear that this was a fight that never entirely went away. The husband was being provocative, claiming his wife made far too much fuss about the hours it took to plan and prepare meals for their family of four, while he himself was emptying the dishwasher on a daily basis and taking the garbage out once a week without any fuss whatsoever.

They didn't let us in to what was happening with all the other tasks it takes to run a household, but the husband's insistence on equating meal-making with dishwasher-emptying made it clear that high levels of resentment were leading to very low levels of appreciation. What's more, by limiting his contributions to the daily running of their home, he was not only controlling who would do what, he was also *taking charge of how those tasks were valued and described.*

· · ·

BELITTLING OR JUST underestimating the household tasks that you are not doing yourself is commonplace. And it matters. It may be a very human weakness to exaggerate the importance of what we are doing while underplaying what others do, but when it is about things that consume as much time as do shopping, cooking and ordinary household maintenance (never mind child care), this will cause serious hurt.

When we discount what other people are contributing to our well-being, we risk making them feel personally discounted also. When lazy gender assumptions come into the picture, it makes things worse. Whether or not both partners are in paid work, most women continue to do almost twice as much housework as their male partner. And new studies show that when women earn more than their husbands, they do even more of the housework, so as not to further offend or confront his masculinity.

That speaks volumes about what is routinely seen as "women's work." In fact, some men will talk about "helping" with tasks that rightly should be shared. It's no surprise then that it is "women's work," as well as the varied emotional and physical tasks associated with care of children, the elderly or the unwell, that seems especially prone to being downplayed. Those tasks are so easy to see when they are *not* done. They are even easier to overlook when they *are* done. And perhaps especially when they are done well.

HOW THINGS ARE DECIDED matters in every partnership. That dynamic demonstrates the power relationship—and each individual's relationship to power—as almost nothing else will.

It can be tempting to concede things that are quite important to you for fear of seeming petty or querulous. It can be tempting, too, to let resentment build until it explodes over something apparently trivial that is one straw too many. A quiet check of how things are being played out—who's deciding what—is always useful, especially when it's done in a spirit of inquiry rather than blame. That also develops the ability to compromise and to see another person's point of view.

The division of practical household tasks is only part of the picture. One person's life and interests being regarded as self-evidently more important than their partner's life or needs is also a power issue. So is the sharing of money.

Sharing power around money means both partners knowing who earns what; acknowledging who has the most access to money-earning time; looking at what unpaid work is needed and who is doing it; giving real value to the emotional care of adults as well as children; discussing and agreeing on how money will be earned, spent and shared.

In many households men are genuinely equal partners emotionally and financially. Some are doing more than their share. But as I watch, look and listen, I see that even for some young men home remains primarily a place to relax and be cared for. And when that doesn't happen, or doesn't happen as they believe it should, they feel entitled to complain. Much of what their mothers did, they quite unself-consciously expect a wife to provide. For many women, by contrast, home is primarily a place of work even when they also have a place of work. And, when things go wrong, they feel they have only themselves to blame.

. . .

HOUSEHOLD responsibilities can't and won't always be evenly divided. That's not the point. What does matter is sustaining some awareness and respect for what each is contributing. It's this respect, particularly, that will profoundly affect the way each person thinks about the other and regards and treats them.

Even the most traditional relationships will benefit greatly from establishing a simple rule: *unless you are willing to take total responsibility for the task under discussion then you have no right to criticize it or comment on it (other than with gratitude).*

HOWEVER POWER is played out within a relationship—gracefully or grudgingly—it will affect the ease and pleasure with which the couple thinks about having, and not having, sex. It is difficult for most women to move easily from being seen as an inadequate, disappointing or "bloody awful" housekeeper, partner or parent to being a highly desirable (and desiring) woman. In fact, I would say that for most women this switch is virtually impossible.

Grievances are not sexually exciting. (Nor is being bored, boring or ignored.) Whatever other foreplay the sexual relationship needs, the most critical is always the respect, love and admiration that is played out consistently, day by day. There are men who believe that tension, even fights, are best resolved in bed. Again, this is far less often true for women. Like it or not, most women remain dependent on a general atmosphere of goodwill and good humor to find and sustain the energy for a sexual life, especially for one that is sensual, fun and mutually rewarding.

In long-term intimate relationships, sexual appetites will wane, flounder, return and not always match. When people want to have more time together for sex, they will need and must have *more time together.* Time to share, to talk, to enjoy one another, to welcome surprises: not always to be cook, cleaner, therapist, parent (to the spouse or to the children).

WHEN IT COMES to issues of power and marital happiness, it is always wise to check your gender assumptions ("Men should always . . . wives can never . . ." "Other women don't. . . ." "Decent husbands can. . . .").

Some of your innermost expectations may be wildly unrealistic. They may also be insulting to the real live person in front of you. This is not a postfeminist age. Sexism remains alive and well even though some of its restrictions have lifted and some of its manifestations have become more subtle.

Sexist assumptions limit men as well as women (although not equally). They may have slipped into the climate and culture of your family without anyone being quite aware of it. What will help is making your own biases and expectations more conscious, reexamining them rather than expecting them always to be met; letting go of what doesn't add to your self-respect or loving care for your partner; and taking up new ideas and attitudes that will better support you both.

Those small acts of restraint, appreciation and kindness restore harmony and commitment. They restore love and happiness, too. And they certainly build it.

Needs at Odds

꧁

A history of our lives could be written through our changing desires. (Longing for an exciting night out may give way to an overwhelming desire for a good night's sleep . . .)

Wanting something or looking forward to an event can give us a sense of purpose and excitement that also transforms the present moment. We risk a dangerous flatness of spirit if there's nothing in our lives to which we can look forward. We also risk agonies of regret if there is something we long to do—yet must constantly postpone.

But what about the situation where we are passionate to take up or try something new and a spouse or partner has their mind set in a quite different direction? When is it reasonable and respectful to assert yourself as an individual? Or must "the good of the relationship" always come first?

A REFRESHED, stimulated partner brings so much to a relationship that it seems almost tragic that anyone would sacrifice that out of mean-spiritedness, lack of trust or a refusal to be inconvenienced. Yet this happens. We also know that each person must flourish individually if a relationship is to prosper. And we know that when one person wholeheartedly wants something, both must take that seriously.

That's all well and good, I can hear you say, but sometimes life (and those living it) refuses to be rational. Sometimes desires emerge or are articulated at the worst possible time. Sometimes it feels impossible to be fair, especially when there are dependent children involved, a whopping mortgage to be paid, or a sense that a safe future must be secured.

WHEN A SERIOUS ISSUE needs negotiating, it helps to pay much less attention to the immediate choices (whether your partner "deserves" to go hiking in the Andes) and far more attention to the emotional patterns that have come to dominate within the relationship.

Such patterns develop incrementally and are often far from conscious. Nevertheless, they dynamically influence how both people will think and react—and how decisions will be made.

Until a crisis threatens it can be hard to identify whose needs usually prevail. Or if one person's agenda has come to be accepted as intrinsically more important than the other's. You may be aware that one of you is more persuasive in articulating your needs—but how does this influence your separate as well as shared agendas? And what happens in the relationship when someone doesn't get their own way? Does either person punish the other one by sulking or getting angry or sick?

A discussion like this might show you for the first time whether both people feel free to express what they want or think—or what constrains them.

. . .

GOING FORWARD, "how we've always done things" is not necessarily the best or only way. Thinking freshly about those fundamental relationship dynamics gives each person a chance to reflect
on their current needs and particularly on how they are expressing
them.

Over the course of a longer relationship it is highly unlikely that
two people's needs or values will always coincide. Perhaps only one
partner wants to give up a high-paying job for a more satisfying life.
Or is dreaming of six months in Kyoto to learn Japanese. Perhaps
only one of you wants a baby—or another baby. One of you may
want a bigger house while the other dreams of a smaller mortgage
and greater simplicity. Perhaps it turns out that one of you has
strong feelings on this new issue, but is willing to concede on something else.

What the issue is, and what is wanted, will matter far less
than the care with which each person's feelings and opinions are
negotiated.

DISCUSSIONS OF THIS KIND depend on careful listening and a
willingness to have your mind or opinions changed. Ancient
hostilities make this kind of negotiation impossible. For it to work
both people must feel listened to, appreciated and understood.

A realistic sense of timing is also crucial. If there are vulnerable
dependants involved, any significant assertion of independence may
have to be dramatically curtailed or postponed. Yet, even in those
less flexible years, most people can still find ways to manage what's
best for their partner, whether or not it's ideal for them. Negotiated

respectfully, and with some concessions on both sides, they may soon find that the long-term benefits far outweigh the short-term upheaval.

Vibrant relationships deepen and mature when two people retain a strong sense of themselves as well as of their relationship. It's exactly this kind of mutual exploration that will reveal what intimacy and individuality can truly mean. This allows for a rich and invigorating life, if not always a predictable one.

Passion and Possession

Passion and possession might seem like two branches of the same tree. And it's true that people gripped by the madness of extreme possessiveness will often claim that their actions are dictated by passion or love. Yet one is never an excuse for the other. No matter how passionate someone feels, they have no right to dominate and control another person. And in predicting the health of an intimate relationship, even hints of such possessiveness should be cause for alarm.

One of the most obvious difficulties with disentangling passion from possessiveness is that it is highly subjective. You might, for example, feel perfectly entitled to call your partner twenty times a day to chat—or to check where they are. You might think it natural to insist that you always socialize with friends or family together. You might press for tiny details of past relationships. You might think it's fine to read your partner's e-mails or journal, listen in on their phone calls or forbid them to have friends of the opposite sex. You might think forbidding is itself permissible.

. . .

NONE OF THOSE BEHAVIORS is loving or reasonable. Possessiveness is driven by insecurity and lack of trust. Both are undermining and when they show themselves in the form of poor boundaries and a need to control, this is itself abusive and is highly likely to lead to relationship breakdown. For that reason alone we should be alert to the seriousness of such behaviors. And yet from the point of view of the person behaving this way, such actions may seem defensible or even natural.

The possessive person may well be highly skilled at controlling the emotional agenda, including how their own motives and behavior are described and interpreted. This frequently leaves their partner feeling unsure about their own perceptions, which makes it vital to understand that possessive, controlling behaviors are irrational and frequently dangerous.

WHAT I AM DESCRIBING is all too familiar. The good news is that it's not always or necessarily hopeless. The possessive, controlling person is often riddled with anxiety or dominated by past experiences of betrayal, perhaps going back to childhood. Often their greatest fear is of being left or abandoned. So before anything else can change they need to see that they are acting *against* their own best interests, because what's most likely to drive a loved one away is not that person's untrustworthiness or disloyalty but their own bleak interpretations and unreasonable behavior.

Even a glimmer of insight will create change. When the possessive partner can see how powerfully fear is influencing their interpretations, they can question how they are routinely describing events and relationships to themselves. This will help them to see how subjective their interpretations are and that they are based on fear, not facts. With help, they can learn to identify reasons to trust rather than to accuse. And, most essentially, they can disentangle their ideas about love from the entirely false belief that they are entitled to control another person.

What's most helpful here is not just for the possessive partner to understand how emotional experiences in the past influence their thinking in the present (although that's a great insight for all of us to have), but also that they can and must find ways to shift their focus away from themselves. This will allow them to notice in a genuine way *the effects of their behavior* on others. And particularly on the person or people they love most.

AFTER ALL THESE YEARS thinking about human behavior and working with a huge variety of people, I can say with confidence that virtually any harmful psychological pattern will change for the better when someone learns to think far less about their own feelings and far more about how their behavior is affecting other people.

Such awareness—and the insights that accompany it—lets you take charge where previously you might have felt helpless. Learning to exercise power positively rather than negatively is literally trans-formative. Many possessive, controlling people blame others for their own feelings and behavior ("If she didn't . . . I wouldn't . . ."). It is courageous as well as liberating to take unconditional re-sponsibility for the *effects* of your emotions and actions. And it's wonderful to discover how possible it is to live more confidently and cheerfully, with increasing kindness, warmth and trust.

Few people want to live like a tyrant. Or with one. Accepting how subjective our fears and judgments are, and accepting that only we can change them, we become more self-responsible as well as more self-aware. Taking other people's well-being seriously is also radically helpful. Positive insight like this will always bring change. And never more so than where love survives—and now has a chance to flourish.

All Grown Up

❀

There can be few relationship breakdowns as sad as that between parents and estranged adult children. With my own children now safely grown up, I know how joyful and deeply rewarding the relationship between adults of different ages can be. You continue to feel tremendously interested in your children's lives. You go on feeling vulnerable for and about them. Yet there is also an increasing experience of ease and mutuality once you are no longer responsible for their daily care.

There is also a welcome sense that you have lots to learn from their contemporary way of looking at the world. Maybe I particularly relish this reframed intimacy because it's not what I had (my mother died far too early; I lived abroad). But I am also aware that in many families where parents are still living, and want that connection, that delightful bonus of parenting is not happening.

In some families the adult children merely tolerate their parents or find them dull. They may avoid them other than when money is needed, or babysitting. In other families adult children create distance by being aggressive or even actively abusive.

There are also parents who continue to treat their adult children like children, even into the "children's" late middle age, making assumptions about them, telling them how they should live or raise their own children, criticizing their religious or philosophical beliefs, and crossing emotional and physical boundaries without the smallest degree of embarrassment or regret.

Parents like that—and they are far from rare—may even insist that their happiness depends on their children's choices. This is blatant emotional blackmail, of course, because what is at risk are not the children's decisions but the parents' need to exert control. Using religion, cultural norms, fear of other people's opinions, money or health issues to manipulate the lives of people you claim to love is immensely harmful. It breeds and feeds resentment. And it destroys any possibility of developing a relationship built on genuine mutuality and respect.

As ADULT CHILDREN grow older and their parents age, there will always need to be significant adjustments on both sides. That's true in any relationship but perhaps with adult children and their parents something else is called for.

The roles of parent and child loom large in our unconscious minds. We might continue to have all kinds of expectations of what or how a parent or child ought to be way past the point when those inner images are appropriate. A poor sense of boundaries, and a lack of respect for the separate integrity of their children, will certainly push some parents to behave inappropriately and intrusively. Those parents may also feel entitled to a level of interest from their adult children that more properly belongs to the adult child's partner or children.

Just as seriously, similar reasons and misunderstandings of the changed roles may cause some adult children to go on resenting and punishing their parents in a kind of perpetual adolescence.

Gripped by their own emotional needs, and seeing their parents only in relation to those needs—and not as distinct, complex individuals—adult children in that situation will often be eager to recall in detail long years of parental failings. This may be their primary inner story: how their parents failed them and how the long shadow of their childhood still lives on.

When that happens, they may find it difficult or impossible to remember or value any of the kinder, more selfless moments that also almost always exist.

THE LOVE BETWEEN adult children and their parents is singularly intimate. To thrive, it depends on an irreplaceable complex history *and* also on lively, loving interactions in the present moment. Most of all, it depends upon an awareness on both sides that each is now an adult and that changes are not just inevitable but welcome.

A long history gives neither side the right to intrude, demand, manipulate or bully—or waste a lifetime wallowing in resentment.

When parental failings have been in the fairly "normal" basket—poor judgments, lack of experience and emotional wisdom, selfish perhaps but not deliberately cruel—it is essential to any claim to maturity that the adult child look for and at the bigger picture.

For their own sake, as well as for the sake of their parents and the extended family more generally, the adult child needs to see their parents not just as parents but also as the flawed, complex, evolving human beings they undoubtedly are. Even when people disagree on significant issues, or feel undervalued or invisible, positive changes can be made. And, with better and less resentful communication, old wounds can be healed.

Just as crucially, parents need to see their adult children not as children only, complete with middle-age spread or grown children of their own, but as beloved yet distinct and separate human beings, with whom love—and ideas *about* love—can to the very last change and grow.

Perfect Lover, True Friend

❀

Having friends and making time for them helps us to feel good about life. Without friends, it's easy to feel empty. And that life beyond work is meaningless. But the gifts of friendship within marriage or a long-term relationship are just as crucial. In the healthiest intimate relationships each partner has shared and individual friends *and* they are able to be real friends to one another.

This means having interests in common beyond what's on TV tonight or who's cooking what or whose turn it is to pick up the kids from child care or to pay the property taxes. Functional parenting and partnering is often the order of the day. But to maintain a loving, vibrant relationship, it's not enough.

WHATEVER INTIMACY you share (or once did), your partner remains a separate person. It is vital to acknowledge this, not least with your interest in their opinions, daily experiences, needs, desires and dreams. With luck, they have a life that extends beyond the four walls of your home and even the beloved people in it. Taking a lively interest in all those aspects of life is part of friendship, within and outside marriage.

This doesn't necessarily mean spending entire weekends lying on your stomach staring through binoculars if your partner happens to be an avid bird-watcher. Or going to every new ballet in town when you don't know a pas de deux from a *grand* plié. It does mean regarding that interest with some respect, noticing what it brings to your partner and meeting their enthusiasm with enthusiasms of your own.

Showing interest is what most of us would do for a friend, often without thinking about it. Yet that open-minded validation—along with routine kindness and good manners—is often quickly lost in a sexual relationship. And how sad that is. After all, we generally think of intimacy as more meaningful than friendship, yet many intimate partners offer each other *less* validation than they give their friends.

INTIMATE FRIENDSHIP and sexual intimacy really are different experiences. Sexual intimacy is far more likely to stir up issues from your forgotten or even unconscious past. It can make you vulnerable and self-questioning and perhaps more than usually self-focused, even while your gaze is apparently on someone else.

In fact, even when you are long past the first heady stages of mutual fantasy ("I've met the *perfect* person!"), your subjective anxieties about intimacy may make it more difficult than it should be to "get" that you should be more and not less sensitive to the one you love. When a lover opens their life and heart to you, and shares their inner world as well as physical love, they are actually risking far more than we do in a fully clothed friendship.

This means that how you think and behave matters *more*—and not less—in an intimate relationship than it does in a friendship.

Respect matters more; boundaries matter more; courtesy matters more; and continuing interest matters far more.

WHEN I WOULD LISTEN to stories from couples in therapy it was clear that what often gets in the way of an intimate relationship is a crowd of unconscious assumptions or demands that have been projected onto the other person: *make me happy*; *give my life meaning*; *know what my needs are even when I don't*; *be perfect*. These can weigh the relationship down heavily, not just because they are unrealistic, but also because they make it harder to see and appreciate what *is* happening and what *is* going well.

Helping people to find ways to articulate their deepest wishes can be a turning point. The conscious mind can be your ally: seeing more clearly what is reasonable and what is not. This is wonderful to know because when those less conscious projections or needs are not and cannot be met, there is often deep disappointment or even rage or outrage. From everything feeling blissful and perfect, the wheel turns to everything feeling hurtful and wrong. Almost no one would confess to harboring those extreme demands. But as couples rage, weep or blame, it's precisely those unrealizable demands that they are living out.

INTIMACY GETS ITS best chance when each person can move from an impossible idealization ("With this perfect person I will have a perfect relationship") to a more genuine sense of who the other is and what an intimate relationship can or even should provide.

A partner should not be a parent. A partner can't make up for the imperfections of our parents, nor should they. Experiencing adult love can be powerfully healing of old sorrows. It is and must be, however, always a different and less self-focused experience.

UNCONSCIOUS DEMANDS can be fierce and, as long as they are not "owned," particularly difficult to meet. Once we recognize any pattern of need and name it, though, it loses much of its power and we can do something about its effects.

This helps each individual to be more self-responsible and more resilient ("Some of my needs *I* can take care of . . . I still have some of the feelings left over from childhood . . . but I can act on them quite differently").

As each person becomes more individually confident and self-aware, this also helps them, as a couple, to appreciate each other very much as friends would. And far from making things less special, this inevitably enhances rather than diminishes a couple's love. It's a relief, always, when people can see their partner separate from them and their most ravenous needs. It's a relief, too, to discover that you no longer need someone else to "save" you.

It supports your intimacy to look for—and find—a more conscious psychological picture. It makes each person more interesting. It engenders respect and confidence, as well as curiosity and appreciation. It also saves couples from retreating into a kind of barren functionalism when most of their explicit communication is about who is doing what, and when.

Deliberately cultivating a loving friendship—and especially the interest and respect we associate with that—plays a vital part in leading us out of the maze of unconscious and unrealistic projections. It supports a healthy separateness while also making togetherness more pleasurable. Validating and encouraging one another on a daily basis, enjoying difference, making allowances, checking on what we are asking for and why: these easy habits reduce the bad times and massively support the good.

In friendship we don't expect to be everything or to get everything. *We focus on what we have.* A similar pattern doesn't diminish the magic of intimacy. It enhances it.

IDENTITY

✺

Make It Happen

✳

Do you have a stylish outfit in your wardrobe waiting for a day that may never come? Do you long to master a skill or another language, yet are always putting it off? Is there a country you have always dreamed of visiting but so far you've been there only in your dreams? And what about the expressive arts? Have you long promised yourself that you will write, sing, dance, put together a family history or take up photography or painting in a serious way "once you have the time"?

"ONCE YOU HAVE THE TIME" may seem as much of a fantasy as "once upon a time." Many of us have a list of postponements matched in length only by our list of dazzling excuses as to why we can't until . . . or how much we would love to . . . if only.

This can apply as much to relationships as to activities. And that's surely even sadder. Perhaps you have some much-loved friends that you often talk about but never quite get around to calling. Or you may long to have a new relationship yet avoid situations where you could possibly meet someone. More seriously still, there may be people from whom you are estranged and you are putting off taking that vital first step toward a reunion. Or perhaps it's a baby you have long wanted, if only the time was right.

ALL TOO OFTEN we promise ourselves that we will do or achieve something because it fits our idea of the kind of person we are rather than because it truly feels essential. After all, most of us discover we have all the time in the world if we are sufficiently motivated. When we fall in love, for example, we find endless time for our new beloved. But back in the prosaic realms of ordinary living, we are more than likely to pick up those same old patterns of postponement and prevarication.

It's when we do at last find ourselves with time to take up the tango, travel to the Galápagos or invite our long-neglected friends or relatives to stay or just for dinner, that we might feel most confronted. Without all those excellent reasons to put something off, we are forced to think hard about how our manic schedules may in fact have been shielding us. We are also forced to ask what it is that we truly want.

It's easy to believe that we haven't time for anything that's not urgent or essential if that's what we are constantly telling ourselves. Less predictably, as long as we are endlessly postponing some of the things we claim to care about—and especially some of the loveliest or most meaningful things—it's easy to prove what an admirably *useful* life we are living. So useful, indeed, that some of our deeper and more complex needs can't get a look-in. While we are preoccupied with running in place, it's also easy to believe that there will always be time to make things right. And that we and those we care about will live forever.

. . .

OUR SELF-CONFIDENCE depends in part on trust that we can make decisions that will enhance our lives, and make them easily and often. Kindness comes in here, too. Leading a useful life is one thing. It also needs to be a life built on kindness, appreciation, concern and engagement if we are truly to honor it.

If there are things that you would genuinely love to do, if you have dreams to realize, friends or family it would give you joy to see or significant rifts to mend, then you owe it to yourself to look hard at what you are postponing, and why. Even in the most demanding lives with young children and paid work, a gentle shift in our priorities is possible. Making time for something that matters adds up to making time for ourselves. Everyone benefits.

Surprisingly often, not much else is needed. What also helps is regarding time and your own deeply held desires and dreams as resources, rather than as the enemy. They are helping to create your life. It's up to you to live it.

Thinking About Readers

Rumor has it that my schoolteacher mother taught me to read long before I went to school. The idea was that she, my father and sister could then get on with their own books in peace. Who knows if that's quite true, but reading has certainly been my most consistent pleasure, protector, educator and illuminator. If stuck, I read labels. Although mostly I insure myself against that awful fate by having several books at hand, assuming that if one is terminally dull I can quickly compensate with another.

What this means is that I cannot remember a time when I didn't treasure what reading could give me. What's more, even as a young reader I was conscious that I felt a genuine intimacy with the writers whose work I loved best. I felt gratitude, too, not just for the discoveries that reading gave me but because surprisingly often I would finish a book feeling personally affirmed or understood, even when the writer's own life or circumstances were significantly different from mine.

In the company of my favorite writers, I felt *met*. What also moved me was how often conversations that began on the page echoed in other areas of my life. As a keen reader, I felt part of a reflective community that wasn't limited by time or place but was sustained by curiosity, diversity, and a need to communicate and understand.

I BEGAN WRITING seriously in my midthirties. By then I had been working in book publishing for most of a decade and for the last five years of that time had been founder and managing director of the London publishers, The Women's Press.

The world of books was thrilling to me but that didn't mean I found it easy to contemplate leaving publishing, and starting to write for a living. Having worked with many gifted writers, I knew firsthand how difficult it is to write originally and well and to sustain that for more than a single book. Many writers don't get better just because they keep on writing. The specter of failure hovers over every dedicated writer, no matter how successful, not least because good writing depends on inspiration and a version of magic that even the most faithful attention to craft won't produce to order.

I feared the elusiveness of that magic. I feared its loss. And I have to face that fear again with each new book.

WHAT I DIDN'T fully grasp as a reader or as a publisher, and perhaps discovered only when I had taken up writing as my central work, was how intimate the relationship with readers is for the *writer*.

Without ever knowing most readers personally, a writer can nevertheless sense and be inspired by them. Writing works best for me when I feel confident that I am writing *for* readers, at least as much as I am writing for myself. I want to understand life with greater subtlety and confidence; I assume you do, too. This demands, of course, that I am able to sense what readers may be looking for by the time each book is completed. Because books take years to write, this can mean anticipating ways of thinking about the big personal and spiritual issues, and trusting that these will be, or will become, of general interest.

It's been deeply stimulating to me to think about readers taking up ideas from my books or articles and finding benefit from them in their own lives. Because my subject matter goes to the heart of readers' lives, as well as my own, nothing encourages me more than when a reader writes or tells me, "That book got me through. . . ." Or, "I always felt you wrote that book for me. . . ." Or, "When you wrote that article on . . . I finally felt understood."

Throughout my writing years, I have imagined you not as a crowd, but as individuals. I have listened closely to the readers I do meet. I have thought about your lives, needs, challenges, sorrows, joys, and unanswered and sometimes unanswerable questions.

I have allowed my sense of you to challenge, sustain and extend me. I have taken long walks in your company, plotting out ideas. At public events and on Facebook, I have met a surprising number of you and will never meet others. But throughout I have been moved to care even more deeply because of your side of this unique writing/reading pact. You—you readers—have allowed me to become an even more passionate and instinctive writer than I would have been without you. I thank you deeply.

Becoming Australian

✿

A few years ago, I became an Australian. Perhaps I was no more of an Australian than I had been the month before or will be a decade from now. Nevertheless, an official transformation did take place. I had my letter from the Minister for Immigration, passed my quiz (not hard), and waved a flag at the delightful citizenship ceremony at our local town hall. The mayor wore her best robes and beamed at us like favored relatives. The brass band played. Lamingtons were served with cups of tea and glasses of sticky cordial. And it was clear with what joy each new citizen was calling Australia home.

I HAVE LIVED in Australia longer now than I have lived anywhere else. The earlier years of my life were divided in roughly two chunks between New Zealand, the much-loved country of my birth, and Europe, where I lived for sixteen years. Those layers remain. But becoming officially Australian came to feel increasingly "right."

My children were born here and are wholeheartedly Australian. Close members of my birth family live here. My writing life was established here. So was my ministry. I now have long friendships and irreplaceable relationships here. What's more, I truly love this country with all the complexities that any authentic love affair implies. I delight in what's best about our national character (hospitality, adventurousness, earthiness, fairness) and am dismayed in a suitably proprietorial manner about what is worst (boorishness, insularity, anti-intellectualism, increasing materialism).

The city in which I live—Sydney—continues to enchant me more than it frustrates me. It is considerably tougher than the city I came to in 1983. It's overdeveloped and underresourced. It costs far too much to live here. Too many of us work ridiculous hours in order to afford it. It's hell for drivers. It's a much worse hell for those who are poor, ill or socially marginalized. Nevertheless, it combines urban excitement with breathtaking bursts of natural beauty and wraps itself around a marvelous variety of experiences.

Making that allegiance more official I don't love my birth country less. I am no less an Anglophile—or Francophile—than I ever was. But I know that Australia has a unique place in my affections.

THROUGH THE WHOLE effortless process, I was powerfully aware what a privilege citizenship is. Australia remains one of the world's safest and most open countries. When we don't like something we may not be able to change it, but we can certainly protest. We have social services that we can afford to take for granted. Bigotry is generally contained. Extremism is disparaged and discouraged. Good humor, kindness and community are still valued.

People risk their lives for freedoms like these. And will continue to do so. Most of us believe those freedoms are our right, but perhaps it is better to see that they are a priceless privilege that we hold safe for one another. Even the idea of Australian citizenship is like a mirage to many. Yet for me, coming to Australia originally with a New Zealand passport and right of entry, it has been an accident of birth, the lottery for which I didn't even have to buy a ticket.

This is not to say that the first years were easy. I missed my friends terribly. I missed those daily points of reference you barely notice until they are gone. I missed my London life and my life in publishing, the world that had taken so long and such effort to establish. I missed all of it intensely and was shocked on a daily basis by how visceral that "missing" was.

Remembering that time, I see again what a different country Australia is when you have lifelong friendships here, when you went to school here, or have family or social networks you can take for granted. But it was far easier for me than for many. I chose to come to Australia and wasn't forced to seek refuge. I came with a partner. I spoke the language (more or less!) and the cultural references were largely familiar to me.

As a young woman I lived in two different countries, Israel and Germany, where I discovered firsthand how easy it is to lose confidence and even your sense of self when your cultural references are different and especially when you don't know the language. Without language and cultural fluency, you become invisible or irritating to others. And you quickly become something of a stranger to yourself.

It is impossible to feel wholly part of any country or to contribute fully to it while standing on the edges looking in. In a nation of migrants, as this one largely is, those of us who are already here need to think hard about where those margins are and what maintains them. We need to think about how to welcome newcomers more practically; how to accept their differences while sharing more generously what we have and what they are seeking. We need policies that acknowledge how crucial communication is to mutual understanding and any real sense of belonging. We need to lobby effectively for far more free, and freely available, English-language classes and, with them, greater clarity about the best of our cultural values.

CITIZENSHIP IS as much about giving back as it is about receiving. Despite our current asylum-seeking tragedies, outsiders continue to think of Australia as a friendly, accepting and tolerant country. As one of Australia's newer citizens, I would say that this is less a compliment than it is a challenge. It's a challenge to governments. But most of all it is a challenge to each of us to live the ideal—and make it come true.

A Big Success at Failure

⚛

In a society that worships success, it's easy to fail. But it's hard to fail well. It is even hard to be sure what "failing well" might mean, although it's likely to include being fairly graceful about it, avoiding bitterness or blame, learning something from it and not allowing it to obliterate your hard-won confidence or sense of self.

We generally associate failure with making a mistake. It seems to reflect on us; maybe it threatens to obliterate us. Yet with many familiar "failures" there may be no mistake at all. You might fail to get a job, for example, but can't change the fact that the interviewer was anyway going to appoint her best friend. You might fail to impress a new date, or to soothe a suffering friend, not because you are hopeless but because they have their own dramas in which you barely feature. Closer to home, your child may fail to get into a desired school or to score the marks you so desperately wanted for her. Or your partner may fail to notice what an effort you have made with your preparations for his return home after a week away. But, again, their stories are complex and are not entirely about you and your desires and dreams.

Are those situations "failures?" Are they mistakes? Should they send you into a spiral of self-blame or go to the heart of your sense of self?

Surely a more realistic and far more encouraging challenge is to see that you are dealing with disappointment, sadness or frustration, rather than failure. How you do that will depend on a number of factors. The occasional frustration in an otherwise rosy life is a quite different proposition from dealing with the latest in a painfully extended series of blows. Indeed, when one disappointment leads rapidly to another, something more than patience is needed. You may need to take an honest look at what you are hoping for—and what you are expecting of yourself and other people.

SOMETIMES our unconscious expectations are totally unrealistic. Indeed, sometimes our *conscious* expectations are totally unrealistic! We may expect so much of ourselves or other people that it's impossible *not* to fail. Our measures of success may also be painfully narrow. And, if we have developed that all too common habit of catastrophizing, this will make any individual disappointment far worse: "If my child doesn't get into the right kindergarten he won't get into a top school, won't be able to get into a great university and will never earn a decent living. And it's all my fault."

We live in a brutal world of shortcuts where crass stereotypes often prevail. Learning that you are not at the center of every drama in which you play some part is crucial to your emotional survival. It also helps to be coolly realistic about whether you are routinely setting yourself up for disappointment and even failure both through your expectations and through the way you describe these painful scenarios to yourself. If you think that's the case, it becomes easier to look at each situation from a more generous perspective.

. . .

THE MORE FAMILIAR forms of failure—doing something badly or letting yourself or someone else down—are also psychologically complex.

A fear of failure, and especially of being "seen" to fail, can be brutally inhibiting for many people. More often than not, that's because they have given to others the power to value their lives or even to make sense of them.

Many people go through life full of anxiety about *what they assume other people are thinking*, scarcely noticing that most people are not thinking about them at all and that the fiercest critic is always lodged in their own mind.

What helps is noticing what you are doing, checking in, and then taking for granted that your assumptions (and fears) are often not based in reality. And even if they are, even if the other person does think you are a complete idiot or not fit to be appreciated or forgiven, you may also learn to see that this judgment, too, is complex and need not guide or determine your own self-worth.

Defying Perfectionism

We all make mistakes. We all do things that we regret (or should). We all let ourselves and other people down. And we are all far more likely to be tolerant of other people's mistakes and human failings when we can get over the horror of our own inevitable imperfections.

For perfectionists, though, making a mistake is not just part of life. It describes and diminishes who they believe themselves to be.

Weeping when your efforts are not admired, obsessing about the small detail that was less than perfect or overlooked, bewailing the mark or two your child didn't get on their test, demanding unrealistic results and admiration on a constant basis or living in fear of what other people are thinking are all signs of galloping perfectionism. And it's never kind. The good news, though, is that changes can be made.

What this means is not reliving that mistake a thousand times, not talking about it endlessly, not beating yourself up for it or blaming someone else, but seeing it clearly for what it is, getting a sense of proportion about it—and moving on.

. . .

WHEN PERFECTIONISM rules your thinking, doing your best is rarely good enough. Beyond doing their best, many perfectionists also want to *be* the best. And be seen to be the best. Yet few of us are "the best" at anything much. And even when we are, that pleasure is fleeting.

It helps to see that being the best at something doesn't make you a kinder, better, happier person. It doesn't justify your existence. It doesn't make life all right. It may assuage your fears briefly, but it can't address the deeper sense of meaning and mattering that every perfectionist will continue to seek.

Loosening perfectionism's hold on you doesn't mean that you won't still try hard or want to succeed. It simply means that your sense of self and inner confidence won't depend on the mirage of a perfect outcome or perfect moment. You will trust yourself more. You will like yourself more. *You will be easier to please* (rather than impossible to please).

Sometimes this will involve getting a bigger picture of your own life's value, establishing a life of greater meaning, questioning how you belong in our shared universe and what you are prepared to give and to offer others. It may also mean quite radically redefining what you think a mistake is, shifting your focus from "tragedy" to "opportunity to learn more." It will certainly mean learning to focus more on the *process* of what you are doing rather than on whether it will lift or lower you in your own or in other people's eyes.

I remember one young woman describing her recovery from anxious perfectionism as giving up a straitjacket that she didn't know she was wearing. Her anxiety had kept her painfully self-focused and kept her life unnecessarily small. It was a delight for her to get over that and not just see but also experience a bigger and more realistic picture.

LIKE ANY unhelpful pattern that involves both thinking and feeling, perfectionism needs consistent unpicking. Noticing its limiting effects is the essential first step. You may need to challenge your most familiar assumptions repeatedly—and calm your worst fears. But you can be confident that, like all expressions of anxiety, perfectionism is driven by your perceptions of reality and not by any fundamental truth. Those perceptions can and will change. And *you can change them.*

Your fears about what other people are thinking will also change as you learn to think more generously about yourself. Most of us are relatively relaxed around other people's slips, not least because they so nicely remind us that we are all human and not robots or saints! That rare person who does delight in others' failings is exhibiting a poor sense of self and should be pitied or ignored, rather than feared.

KNOWING THAT you are prepared to risk living a larger, more robust and comfortingly imperfect life is a vision worth pursuing. Not being perfect means allowing yourself the luxury of being a learner, a beginner, a novice. It promotes courage and redefines "effort." Often the most stimulating opportunities extend our capabilities or exceed them. Taking them on, we do indeed risk falling flat on our face. But we might also fly. And even if we do fall or fail, that will always matter far less than our willingness to rise up to try again.

Widening the Circle

Feeling left out is something that even the most popular people dread. The image of a child standing alone in a crowded playground, without the protection of friends, haunts many adults. In adulthood there are countless parallels.

Feeling left out seems to go to the heart of the way we feel about ourselves, arousing fears of abandonment even if the situation is relatively trivial.

This makes it vital for our personal and our social well-being, as well as for our moral and emotional intelligence, to know that *we can take charge of including other people in our activities*, bringing them in and making them feel comfortable and valued. We need to know that we are capable of overcoming our self-consciousness to put others at their ease. And we need to be able to do this even if we assume that other people have a far easier time than we do making friends, feeling part of things or fitting in.

An easy sense of belonging is essential to feeling safe. Whatever our age or status, we want that sense of belonging. And we remain free to offer it. This simple recognition contributes something exceptionally precious to our collective well-being. It also puts us in a powerful rather than powerless frame of mind. It lets us act with poise in situations where we might otherwise feel overwhelmed. It expands our world. It makes the world a more interesting place.

Nevertheless, there will always be some people who are overwhelmed by their shyness or self-consciousness or their concerns that reaching out to others will make them appear weak, needy or vulnerable.

Even more disastrously, some of the most common and familiar power plays in our society depend on *not* including other people, on a kind of us/them mentality that is hurtful and sometimes dangerous. What this amounts to are various forms of shunning, which give one group a sense of belonging, always at the expense of others.

Those are socially learned behaviors driven by attitudes that can flourish only if they are seen as desirable or inevitable. They depend on a grave misunderstanding of what personal power and responsibility mean. And they benefit no one. In fact, as any schoolgirl could tell us, wherever shunning or exile hovers, there will always be an undertow of fear that makes belonging an untrustworthy, uncomfortable experience.

YOUNG OR OLD, the capacity and willingness to think about others and include them makes a profound difference to our confidence and sense of self. We see this with the child at preschool who is relaxed enough to share. Or with the brave schoolgirl who defies the tyranny of the "in" group to invite someone less conformist to sit with them at lunch. Or with the boy who refuses to condemn a classmate because he is in some way different. Or with the adult at a party who keeps an eye out for people standing on their own. Or with the colleague who's willing to take the time to show new-comers around a workplace or help them with an unfamiliar task.

In so many situations a simple act of thoughtfulness can make all the difference between someone feeling like an outsider, with all the agonies that can produce, or affirmed and respected. But the benefit is never only to the other person. Thinking and behaving thought-fully also and always benefits the giver.

I would go so far as to say that feeling included—and helping others to feel included—will determine whether we see the world as essentially friendly or hostile. And whether we see ourselves as essentially powerless, or powerful.

The more insecure we feel, the more likely it is that we will *underestimate* our own personal power and *overestimate* other peo-ple's feelings of confidence and security. We will spend too much time worrying about being left out. We will spend too little time considering whether and how we can turn this situation around.

It still amazes me how many people complain about feeling left out or overlooked yet never consider how they could so readily save others from similar experiences. I have spoken to many children as well as adults about these critical issues of inclusion and exclusion. Most are highly sensitive to the topic, yet relatively few see that the most effective way to help themselves is to help others.

WE OFTEN FEEL ashamed as well as uncomfortable about our anxieties or shyness. It's tempting to believe that virtually everyone else has an easier time feeling part of things than we do. Yet being realistic about our own insecurities can help us see how much we share with other people. And what we can do about it.

Honesty about our own social vulnerability is the best possible catalyst for action. It can give us the courage to be proactive even when we find this hard. Acknowledging our power to bring other people in rather than leaving them out is brilliant for our self-esteem. It's also brilliantly distracting from the dreary inner monologue that tells us everyone else is far cleverer, better liked and more appreciated than we are. And has far more friends.

INCLUDING OTHERS is a win-win situation. It's great for them. It's great for us. Some children, like some adults, are naturally attuned to other people's well-being. They are society's treasures. We can all learn from them.

Not Just Today, Every Day

❧

Ernest Holmes, who died in 1960, was the author of a key book called *Science of Mind*, and also founder of the Religious Science movement, now widely influential among serious spiritual seekers in the United States. Wisely, Holmes pointed out, "We cannot lead a choiceless life. Every day, every moment, every second, there is a choice. If it were not so, we would not be individuals."

Our most significant choices are made on a daily basis. And are probably far more often made around the constancy of small matters than the occasional big drama. Each day, for example, we will find ourselves in situations where we could be a little less or a little more kind. We will find ourselves speaking to ourselves in the privacy of our own minds harshly—or encouragingly. We will find ourselves paying attention to what makes us most anxious. Or to what will strengthen us.

Taking responsibility for the choices we make is the foundation of genuine self-confidence and resilience. It's intrinsically empowering. It also gives us a real sense of how we can control and choose our attitudes, even when we can't always choose the events that happen or the outer consequences of those events.

. . .

IT TAKES INSIGHT and courage to grow kinder on a daily basis. Often a sharp word rises all too easily to our lips, or a burst of exasperation. Or perhaps our specialty is coldness . . . or a refusal to be truly pleased or satisfied by anything.

Getting over old habits of emotional restriction demands that we recognize them and choose differently. But the rewards are immense. Making a commitment to a kinder life—and trusting that we can achieve it—helps us to disentangle some of our confusion about what we can or perhaps should require of others. And what they should, or should not, put up with from us.

Doesn't it seem obvious that we should expect their very best behavior—and greatest kindness—from the people who claim to love us? And that we would want to offer the people we love our best behavior and greatest consideration and kindness in return? Yet one of the countless paradoxes of the human condition is that so many of us offer the worst of ourselves to the people we claim to love best.

That's bad enough. On top of that, though, we often expect those very same darlings to put up with our outbursts, our sulking, our less-than-fascinating complaints, our self-absorption or our unwillingness to share tasks fairly, or make time for them that is enjoyable and uplifting, *because we claim to love them.* (And, yes, sometimes the reverse is also true. Sometimes we suffer because of the assumptions others make about us, all in the name of love.)

KINDNESS DISALLOWS those kinds of excuses! And occasional or fair-weather kindness is also not an excuse for behaving indifferently or disrespectfully much or any of the time.

The health of your relationships, your connections with others and your confidence in your own self all depend upon *noticing* that you are influencing others constantly through your actions and attitudes. You are lifting their spirits, supporting and affirming them, making their lives more joyful and meaningful—or you are not.

Again, this doesn't mean becoming a slave to the needs of those around you or losing your vital identity as an independent person. It may mean asserting yourself more confidently. It may mean thinking far more strategically and creatively about your daily challenges. It may mean cultivating greater good humor and making much more time for pleasure and agreement with friends, fellow workers and family. It will almost certainly mean growing your capacities for empathy: letting yourself consciously realize that their needs for kindness are very much like your own, and that the small daily choices that take you in a kinder or less kind direction make a huge difference to them. And make a matching difference to you.

It also means noticing in a real way what freedom means to you: the freedom to choose, the freedom to choose wisely. To paraphrase Holmes now and extend his thought: *We cannot lead a choiceless life. Every day, every moment, every second, there is a choice. If it were not so, we would not have the gifts of consciousness, self-awareness and self-responsibility that make us truly human.*

Being Women

✵

As I write this, listening to sublime eighteenth-century music on my twenty-first-century iTunes (it's Andreas Scholl and Barbara Bonney singing Pergolesi's *Stabat Mater*, since you ask, not coincidentally a piece inspired by and dedicated to Mary, the mother of Jesus), there are people all around the world waking up ready to pray, "Thank God I was born a man."

There are also people earnestly praying, even as you read this, that in the next life they will return as a man to speed their path to enlightenment. And in even more familiar (for most of us) cultural contexts, there are countless people who quite unself-consciously assume that their maleness not only gives them privileges but is itself a privilege.

FOR ALL THAT, and despite the gender inequities with which we are so familiar, there is much to celebrate about being a woman. So perhaps the prayer that I would choose to have on my lips is that more women would relish and treasure their gender: that this would add to rather than detract from their self-confidence and emotional well-being; that it would inspire them to discover firsthand how great it can be to see the world through women's eyes and experience the world through a woman's sensibility—with all the variety that suggests.

I would like to pray, too, that women in general would support other women far more routinely and generously. And draw their self-confidence at least in part from the very gifts that their gender brings. I'd need to add to that a prayer that women would envy and emulate men far less, and take with far greater equanimity some of the biological challenges that come with womanhood.

Living in the body of a woman, I long for women to *love* their bodies far, far more and to see that where there are distinctive features about being a woman, the good far outreaches the bad.

MY OWN TWENTIES and thirties were lived out in the midst of a sexual revolution that turned on its head almost every assumption about gender that for many had seemed natural or irrefutable. That revolution—and it was a revolution, for all its failures—was at least as much about valuing yourself as a woman as it was about work, education, health, parenting, sexuality and social choices.

How tragic then that decades later so many women, including young women, continue to struggle with the most fundamental issues of appreciation, confidence and self-acceptance. This makes individual women's lives far less uplifting than they might be. And it's difficult to support girls and other women to the best of your ability when you are unsure about the value of your own life or feel deeply ambivalent about something as basic as your gender. It is also difficult to make wise relationship choices when you are starving for approval not from the people who are most like you but from those who, in terms of gender and perhaps intrinsic power, are least like you.

MYRIAD BODY IMAGE, eating and anxiety disorders loom large on our social landscape. Fat has never ceased to be a feminist issue and the social pressures on women to be thin, weak and physically insignificant have never been greater. I heard fashion commentator Lee Tulloch talk on the radio recently about a young model who had dropped dead in Europe after eating "nothing but green leaves" for several months. Her death is appalling. But it is just as shocking that women collectively don't rise up and declare this thinness fetish to be the total farce and misogynistic sadism that it is.

We care so much about what goes into our mouths, so how ironic is it that we are literally swallowing the lie that the value of our lives is related to our weight? Or that we become more lovable or more beautiful when we resemble a puny adolescent boy, rather than aiming to look like the strong adult woman most of us are.

I HAVE BECOME more cautious than I once was about wading in with emphatic generalizations on the complex realities (and shifting subjectivities) of gender. Nonetheless, it is still possible to suggest that women remain markedly vulnerable to issues of appearance and acceptance because women—far more often than men— continue to look outside themselves for approval, security and even for their sense of self.

Young women tell me with painful exasperation that they are judged by both women and men in their own age group far more harshly and superficially than men are. "Even flabby, unfit men will criticize or disparage women they see as fat," one twenty-three-year-old woman told me. "They don't seem to get the contradiction that they are expecting women to conform to ideals of magazine beauty even when they don't." And she added, "We are talking about guys who are in professional jobs, working with these women as colleagues and sometimes having them as their boss or manager yet still going on about their weight or whether they drink too much or don't look or behave in conventional ways."

There is a painful irony to this because younger women are, in general, more intuitive and savvy than younger men. Nevertheless, needing validation from the outside and especially from men, and giving issues of appearance a significance they don't deserve, women continue to be vulnerable in ways that men will rarely understand. Their qualities of character, their education and achievements, and especially their values can seem to many women to count for nothing when someone else discounts or rejects them on the basis of appearance.

"When a man rejects me I feel like I am no one," is how yet another clever, lovely young woman expressed it to me. And I didn't know whether I most wanted to weep or scream that in twenty-first-century life, young and sometimes not-young women remain far more likely than men to give away their power to others: especially the power to judge whether and how their lives matter.

THROUGH ALL the different stages of life, girls and women continue to need every possible encouragement to claim their gender as an asset. As long as our public culture remains carelessly sexist, ageist and obsessed with its anxious vanities, they need continuing support to define what it means to be a woman—*and to look like one.*

Women can be other women's worst enemies, living out their own insecurity and self-hatred by projecting that negativity onto others, then cutting them down. But that's never the whole story. Contemporary women also have truly exceptional capacities to network, befriend, strategize, encourage—and create the positive changes so necessary for each new generation.

ONE OF THE MOST valuable and persistent insights from that long-ago sexual revolution is that it is impossible to grow in self-confidence and well-being without liking and trusting the meaning we give to gender in our own lives.

We may not want to get down on our knees each morning to express our relief that we have been born in the body of a woman (if that's the case). But when it comes to these crucial issues of self-worth and what that's based on, women can and indeed must be each other's advocates. Women must be each other's most trustworthy friends. And women must find ways to value and befriend themselves.

Supporting other women to value themselves as women, a woman cannot fail also to support herself. This takes nothing from men. In fact, it eases relations between the sexes and makes them more truthful. And everyone benefits.

Too Little Feminism?

✺

Whenever women or girls push the boundaries of acceptable behavior—self-harming, harming others, picking up or taking up the worst of "male" behaviors—feminism gets blamed. But my hunch is that the problem is not too much feminism, but far too little.

More accurately, it may be a lack of understanding of what women set out to achieve in the name of feminism (or, rather, the many "feminisms").

GAINING GREATER CHOICE and autonomy, it was always predictable that some women would prove to be as ruthless in the workplace or in politics as the most ruthless of men; that some women would be as sexually driven and voracious in their personal lives as some men; that some women would abandon or neglect their families, friends or even their children as some men always have. And that some women would behave appallingly in public and in private when social constraints on women became looser.

Perhaps these are the behaviors that caused one female commentator to write: "Mutual respect between the sexes, romance and a legacy of chivalry by men entranced by the feminine mystique have been trashed in the name of female equality and sexual liberation."

LEAVING ASIDE the historical reality that "mutual respect" was often sustained at great cost to individual women, especially when it depended upon women conforming to a narrow, male-defined vision of how they ought to behave, and that "chivalry" and entrancement with the "feminine mystique" did not protect countless women from emotional or sexual abuse, severe limitations on how they could earn income for themselves or their children, or just everyday silencing and disparaging—leaving all that and much else aside, such a statement reveals an almost total misunderstanding of what feminism was once about. And perhaps still is.

AS I REMEMBER IT (and I was there), the guiding freedom that underpinned all the necessary legislative changes was the essential realization that being a girl or a woman was not something to mourn or regret. It was not a reason to accept less, say less or to be less. It was not a reason to be less educated or to earn less. It was not a reason to accept contempt for women or trivialization of their specific concerns as "natural" or "inevitable," as it still is in some cultures, and within some organizations in all cultures. It was not an intrinsic disadvantage when it came to self-respect or self-determination. Nor was it reason to abandon or dishonor the wonderful qualities traditionally associated with women. In fact, it gave every reason to see those qualities—especially the valuing of human relationships— as the strengths they are, bringing them into workplaces, communities and public discourses and spaces; arguing for their validity for women and men alike.

This was a crucial switch in perception that had to begin on the inside: from the way each girl or woman saw herself *and* her place in the wider world.

Taking her measure from the inside out was essential to what was called consciousness-raising. From time immemorial, women had learned to draw their feelings of self-worth from outside themselves and particularly from the ways that men perceived them. Yet as long as it was men's approval or attention that counted most, and as long as women as well as men regarded being a woman as a limitation, women and girls remained vulnerable. They were vulnerable to the way men thought about them; they were even more vulnerable to how they saw themselves.

What the new feminist thinking made brilliantly clear was that the respect that mattered had *first to begin within women themselves*. It also had to extend to one another. To think well of yourself *as a woman*, you had also to rethink what being a woman means and could mean. You had to affirm other women and not see them as competitors and untrustworthy. Or as intrinsically less interesting or less treasured than men.

Many women made those changes. Many more women benefited from those changes. Yet the way women routinely see and describe themselves remains precarious.

THE SEXUALIZATION of ever younger girls, a lack of support by some women for other women in the workplace and the media, women's exhaustion as they juggle "men's" jobs with traditional social and family responsibilities, a continuing obsession not with good health but appearance, frightening levels of eating disorders, sexual risk-taking, drug and alcohol abuse: this cries out for more feminism, not less.

Or perhaps it cries out for a more truthful understanding that greater choices for women will translate into *better choices made by women* only when women's negative behaviors are seen as a (curable) lack of healthy support for themselves and others, just as men's are, rather than as a terminal failure of feminism.

_____

The Great Divide

Perhaps it's parenting that shows up the continuing gender divide in its starkest forms. Across the Western world women still occupy far too few top corporate and government positions. They own just a tiny portion of the world's wealth. Despite some key appointments, they are poorly represented in virtually any forum where power matters. But few things shock individual contemporary women more than the realization that for almost every one of them parenting is a constant occupation or preoccupation while for the majority of fathers, parenting—or the responsibilities that come with it—remains far more fluid.

When a woman asks her partner for *help* with their children, or routinely fills in because "something crucial has come up" at his office, or praises him because he's caring for his own children a few hours a week or has managed to remember a medical appointment other than his own, or comprehends that *she* is where the parenting buck stops and where the blame begins, she is learning firsthand that around parenting, at least, many women and men barely live on the same planet.

. . .

MEN CAN'T and should not be solely blamed. Countless men are simply living out their unconscious assumptions—reinforced every day in our public culture as well as in our homes and businesses— that their time is intrinsically "more important" than women's. And that it is far easier and more "natural" for women to adjust to the constant vigilance that parenting demands (paid work or not), than it is for men to adjust to helping, virtually regardless of who is earning what.

Men also can't be entirely blamed—because women collude with them. The gender inequity when it comes to parenting and running the house, cooking, shopping, laundry, etc., costs many women dearly, but it may also give them some measure of control or power, even while it leaves them ragged and financially vulnerable.

THOSE GENDER assumptions rarely appear before children are born. Once they are born, those assumptions are lived out in the hothouse that is contemporary parenting—often with incredulity and blame on both sides.

It's worth taking it for granted that even if gender issues are not part of your everyday thinking or conversations, they nonetheless carry a great deal of power. Because these issues affect our maturity and identity, inflexible ways of thinking and judging can cost women and men a great deal in terms of psychological well-being. They can also diminish some of the joy that we might have in our children and in ourselves as parents. Care is needed, therefore, in observing our choices and behavior, particularly in our least guarded moments. Good humor is needed, too, and confidence that changes can be made when needed, in both attitude and response.

In fact, how these unconscious assumptions and conscious resentments are brought to awareness and negotiated will be crucial. It might even determine whether a couple will survive the rigorous years of parenting to make a rewarding life together. Or if they will join the nearly 50 percent who cannot make it.

As WITH every other actual or possible crisis in an intimate relationship, honest, thoughtful, *nonblaming* communication is needed. It's extremely tempting to fall into patterns of self-righteousness, bitterness, martyrdom or blame. But when either men or women are blamed for the shortcomings of their entire gender, as well as for their own individual failings, little can be achieved.

In that atmosphere appreciation for what *is* happening, what each is already doing, and what *is* going well, can easily go out the window.

Couples need to be honest with one another about what they can and will contribute to the bigger parenting picture. They need to notice and acknowledge what they are leaving to their partner. They need to inquire whether this is acceptable or fair, rather than simply assuming that this is "the way things ought to be."

Writing checks is far less arduous than caring for little children. Or big ones. Whether one or both parents are in paid employment, it is worth reviewing who is paying for what. And, again, what assumptions are being made about the costs—emotional as well as financial—of the family's care.

Parenting demands high levels of cooperation and compromise.

And truckloads of flexibility, patience and kindness. Treating each other appreciatively, affirming one another as parents, constantly checking in to see what you are taking for granted and what extras you yourself could be doing, are just the most basic first steps in creating a culture of parenting that is sustainable. Just as essential is the absolute, unconditional *banning of criticism*.

When or if you are unhappy about something, see that as a *shared* problem for which you need *shared* and equitably negotiated solutions. Exhausted parents have no energy to waste on blaming.

PARENTS WHO are prepared to go a step further and check their *un*conscious assumptions also will be well rewarded. This might mean noticing what you believe men—or women—"ought" to be able to juggle or achieve. (Your niggling criticisms, even when unexpressed, will provide the clues.) It might mean becoming more aware of when you are comparing your partner to other people (whose lives you probably know far less about than you think), or to your own parents and what (from a child's perspective) you believe each of them achieved.

WHEN A COUPLE has been "everything" to each other, the adjustments to these stark new roles as parents can be surprisingly tough. This is widely known. Nonetheless, many couples sincerely believe that for them it will be different.

Communication is, again, essential. So is constant and constantly mutual appreciation. If loving partners are to become loving parents, new levels of maturity will be required from each. Every moment of a woman's life is changed once she has a child. A man's understanding of this helps. What is far more helpful, though, is if he, too, can see parenting as a unique opportunity to grow in love and selflessness, adding to his repertoire of inner strengths and outer achievements one of the toughest and most humbling—yet certainly the most eternally rewarding.

Vive les Différences!

O ne of the most striking distinctions between fundamentalism (in all its varieties) and contemporary liberalism (in its many varieties) are the ways in which gender is regarded and lived out.

To a man, and whatever the religion or culture, religious-fundamentalist males draw strength and meaning from their perceived superiority to women and what they claim as their God-given right to control women's lives.

Denying women an education and independence, monitoring their clothing, demeanor and conduct, and employing coercion and violence as weapons of gender destruction, are mere basics in twenty-first-century religious-fundamentalist life.

But what's often overlooked in this chilling scenario is not just that such thinking literally imprisons and humiliates women but that it also degrades and dehumanizes men. No one can exercise that kind of unjust power over other human beings without compromising their own decency and peace of mind.

As dark as that picture is, however, and with all the agonies it causes, it does let us see with inescapable clarity how dependent men and women are for their emotional well-being and safety on looking way beyond limiting gender clichés and stereotypes. To feel good about themselves, they need to regard their own *and* the "opposite" sex with interest and respect. This has to include a lively appreciation of difference as well as sameness, taking pleasure in gender distinctions rather than using them to shore up any kind of assumed superiority or inferiority.

GENDER PLAYS a central part in how we think about ourselves and respond to others. It's the first question someone asks when a baby is born: "Is it a boy or a girl?" It crucially determines how we will regard and respond to other people. Nevertheless, how we actually live out our maleness or femaleness may depend almost as much on how we think about gender as on gender itself.

This doesn't mean there are not significant gender differences or characteristics. Anyone who ever thought they could raise their children in a gender-neutral way learns that quickly (as I did!). But even where gender is defined, other differences between people will also count.

Personality, race, sexuality, education, values and beliefs all contribute to that crucial sense of identity, of "This is who I am." They are all powerful influences when it comes to shaping what we believe to be "self" and also "others." Gender affects those dimensions too, but it's not everything. Talent, character and wisdom can all transcend gender and even the most rigid social conditions. Just as wonderfully, human beings remain constantly surprising.

. . .

THE IDEA THAT one gender is intrinsically superior to the other is as outdated as the notion that any race, culture or religion is intrinsically superior to all others. Even so, these are remarkably new, unfinished ideas in terms of human history and our shared social evolution.

Perhaps it is no surprise then that our changes in behavior or in thinking are sometimes slow catching up. Almost all of us will feel trapped at times by limited perceptions. The most encouraging sign on the horizon is that whatever gender is coming to mean for each individual it will reflect and influence an ever-expanding range of characteristics and also choices. Not all of these characteristics will match familiar gender associations, although some may. What matters is that it is increasingly normal for people to be questioning and *challenging their own thinking wherever it limits them*. And discovering how this benefits them as well as others.

THIS IS UNLIKELY to mean that women and men will become more "the same." What seems likelier is that our ideas about gender will continue to change, and greater awareness of choice around all our behaviors will dominate. Perhaps we will more routinely identify which traditional gender characteristics we are keen to develop, which we will quietly modify or drop, and which magnificent differences we will note, cheer and celebrate. *Vive les différences!*

Instinct and Intuition

H ave you ever made a truly awful decision? I know I have (more of them than I care to remember, in truth). And did you then berate yourself because at some level you did know what you were getting into—but did it anyway? Just as crucially, have you ever done something for no reason that you can fathom, only to find that it has rewarded you exceptionally?

I've been thinking a great deal about instincts and intuitions lately and how often we neglect to pay sufficient attention to these exceptional capacities. Perhaps this is preoccupying me in part because I have spent time with several new mothers and can see how necessary it is for them, as it is for all parents, to get into a new relationship with their instincts as well as their babies. Feeling more aligned with their inner "knowing," and more confident in it, they will judge what's best for their babies in ways that a book or another person, however expert, could never match.

INSTINCT IS ONE of the ways in which we are at least somewhat similar to animals. But with our gifts of self-awareness we have far greater choices than any other species about how we will use those

instincts and especially how we will assess what our instincts seem
to be telling us.

From the first moments of life we are driven and protected by a
complex range of instincts, most of which we barely need acknowledge consciously. Our instincts to eat, drink, cry, respond, sleep,
explore, desire and give love are all essential for survival. Yet when
we think about getting through life and taking the best possible
care of ourselves we often take less notice than we should of those
gifts.

OUR INSTINCTS (or intuitions) often warn us of situations where
everything is not as it seems. Yet how easy it is to override them
with our so-called rational mind. A friend introduces you to her
new man, who seems perfect on paper and is charming to you.
Despite that, there's something about him that makes you squirm.
You can't put your finger on it, yet months or even years later you
hear from your hurt and humiliated friend that your initial unwelcome hunch was painfully correct. Or what about that financial
adviser who comes highly recommended? He leaves you feeling
somewhat uneasy but you invest with him anyway as his credentials
are so impressive. Two or twenty years later, your bank balance tells
a sorry story.

Doesn't that make it even more impressive when, despite the
caution of your rational mind, you do follow your instincts even at
the risk of being wrong? You leave work early to pick up your child
from the nursery, only to find that she has a temperature no one has
yet noticed. You refuse a promotion for no reason that you can explain and a month later a much better opportunity presents itself.
You spend the whole day at a nursing home with your elderly father

but just as you are leaving for home you return for yet more time with him—and before dawn the following day he quietly dies.

ANYONE WHO LIVES with animals knows how finely tuned their instincts are, warning us of unfriendliness or danger and also showing their concern by staying close when someone is ill, sad or grieving. Pets can also teach us to tune in to what we most need when we are fearful or unwell.

Hob was a beloved Russian Blue cross male cat who was part of our family for more than seventeen years. When he was badly injured many years before his death he spent weeks of his painful convalescence sitting on my meditation cushions. He hadn't chosen them as a place to sit before; nor did he later. (That story also says a lot about the power of meditation to imbue the surrounding atmosphere with peace.) And when Hob was facing the end of his long life that same magnificent cat spent more and more time in our pantry, needing to be close to the kitchen and its hum, but in quiet darkness. On the day before he died he emerged from the pantry and came into the bright light of the courtyard, carefully licked our other darling cat clean, and then lay with his head on my feet so that he could thank me for the love our entire family had given him and I could thank him for the unconditional love he had given us.

ANIMALS' SURVIVAL depends on their instincts. But most of us are far less confident about using our instinctive reactions or intuitions. Our unique cognitive capacities are so precious to us that rather than seeing how interdependent those different abilities are, we tend to undervalue or ignore our instinctual promptings.

This makes it quite fascinating that many people who are effective leaders and decision makers, or genuinely inventive, say that they make their most significant choices fast and instinctively. Almost all truly original inventions or calculations depend as much on instinct and intuition as they do on formal analysis. And so do the decisions we make on our own and others' behalf. The moments when we do successfully "sniff the air" and "follow our noses" are often deeply memorable. Equally, it may only be when a situation has turned out horribly that we become willing to admit that we "knew" something was wrong and should have acted differently.

IN EVERYDAY LANGUAGE we talk not just about following our noses but also about gut feelings. Those are the mysterious moments when it seems your body knows more than your mind does. Whether it is questions about your health, child rearing, choices at work, love affairs or a vast range of everyday decisions, it's easy to observe how your body relaxes and expands in the face of some inner urgings and tenses and contracts in the face of others.

Trusting our instincts, and tuning in to our intuitions and the feelings they evoke, takes practice. It also takes courage. It certainly doesn't mean setting aside analysis or good sense. Sometimes you will be completely wrong. But there will also be times when you are entirely right. As with any other ability, this one rapidly improves with use, curiosity and reflection.

CHILDREN AND
THEIR PARENTS

✺

Calm Children, Happy Parents

Lots of public parenting goes on over the summer. Family groups spend hours at the beach or hanging out with friends in public parks. These are probably some of the best times of the year for many families. Less rush, fewer demands, looser schedules bring an ease that benefits parents as much as children.

But watching children and their parents over this past summer, I see that even in these easier weeks many parents are struggling with some basic issues. How could this be otherwise? The average age for first-time mothers has just tipped to the far side of thirty. Whatever else they packed into the years before their first child arrived, there was probably precious little time spent with children. And, even if there had been, spending time with other people's children hardly begins to prepare you for the awesome task of caring for your own.

ONE OF THE MOST pressing issues for parents of young children is the vexed one of maintaining routines and keeping children relatively calm and happy. We live in a wondrous world that is also rushed, competitive and tiring. We ask too much of ourselves.

We regard ourselves as rich in many currencies, but not in time. We feel and we are frazzled. This makes us more rather than less confused about how to keep our youngest children calm, confident and happy. No wonder then that we often do what seems easiest in the short term, what gives us a few minutes' respite or what "seems to work," even when we know it doesn't.

It is possible to take a longer view. But let me say at once how wary I am about expert advice when it comes to children. Perhaps only your child's other parent knows your child like you do. If you let them, your own instincts and experiences will tell you more than any book can. In my experience, the totally confident seldom turn out to have children of their own. Or they have children but are supported by a retinue of human wonders: loving partner, their own parents, a fabulous nanny, and so on. In other words, they come from a different planet from the messy place where most of us live.

My list, therefore, is of the humbled-parent variety: hard-won insights, for what they are worth.

1 Establish routines

And mostly stick to them. Children flourish when there are rhythms to the day, every day. External order helps them to "order" themselves internally. Any loss of spontaneity is more than compensated for by greater ease and contentment.

2 Have dinner early

Six o'clock is a fine time for dinner. This is tricky if you have to collect your children from a child-care center after work, but make simple early eating (and bed) the top priority and let everything else wait. Whenever possible, eat together. No television, phones or electronic gadgets. Just family, food and time for one another.

3 Limit the choices you offer

It works well to say, "It's time for your bath," rather than inviting your two-year-old to decide whether she would like her bath before or after dinner, with or without bubbles or for five minutes or six.

4 Say no when you need to

If you must explain, keep it brief. "It's not safe." "We've had enough treats today." Setting limits helps to make a child feel secure. Douse tantrums with disinterest.

5 Talk less

Children can quickly feel overloaded or invaded by too much talk, especially when it's top heavy with opinions and instructions. Long explanations confuse the issue and are rarely needed. The exceptions are when a child asks for more information or is genuinely engaged in a conversation with you. Ten reasons why you need to go home from the park and make dinner are probably nine too many. We mean well but risk being confusing or boring. "Talk less and listen more" works for all relationships; children are no exception. Overtalking expresses our own anxiety. It adds to theirs. Don't withdraw into silence! But if they want lengthier explanations, they'll ask for them.

6 Encourage lots of play

Ideally play is sensual, companionable and physical. Sand, water, mud; building houses from pillows and rolling on the floor; singing, painting, cooking every day; reading and more reading; making up stories; creating gardens; "writing" books: anything that involves the body and engages the senses will delight children and wake them up imaginatively. Give yourselves time to revel in the natural world. (Just think how differently tired children are when they come home from a day at the beach, camping or exploring, versus when they have been worn out at a shopping mall, theme park or entertainment center.)

7 Maintain your patience and good humor

This means limiting stress, not working late routinely, getting enough rest and feeling inwardly spacious enough to enjoy parenting. The greatest gift you will ever give your children is your loving presence. To achieve this, you must care for yourself.

8 Create small rituals of beauty

Make a small ceremony of hello and good-bye. Take a few moments before a meal to appreciate the food and company. Light candles even when it's "just us." Have a small sacred space in each child's room where you put things important to them, including family photos. Invite people to your home and demonstrate that company is welcome. Say a few words together of appreciation for the day before bedtime. Be unafraid to pray with your children and to compose spontaneous prayers together.

9 Be appreciative

And notice how much there is to appreciate even on a hard day. (But don't force this cheerfulness when children are feeling hurt, upset or confused. At those times, *listen*.) If yours is a two-parent family, it's a joy beyond words for children to hear each parent express their appreciation of the other one. If it is a single-parent family, resist any temptation to disrespect the other parent. Appreciate friends and extended family also.

10 Listen when your child confides in you

These moments are golden. The quality of your listening matters far more than your comments. Resist giving advice too quickly. With older children, ask if they would like to know what you think rather than foisting your opinion on them. Respect their boundaries, their differences from you, their distinct worldview.

11 Treat your children courteously

There is no other way they will grow in self-respect or be genuinely courteous to other people.

12 Tell them every day that you love them

Show them through your interest and attitudes how glad you are to be their parent.

Fathers

Motherhood has probably been the single most decisive fact of my life (being my mother's daughter; being mother to my own two children). And this makes me more rather than less interested in the challenges fatherhood offers to contemporary men.

It's hard to believe that fathering as a distinct feature of manhood began to get the attention it deserves only within the past few decades. The pivotal role that fathers play within families was of course thought and written about long before that, but often somewhat indirectly, with some of the most transparent insights emerging through novels and plays.

Feminists are often criticized for playing down the importance of fathers and playing up the problems. Yet it was the careful unpicking of "natural" gender roles, primarily by feminists, and their insistence on how crucial loving fathers are to children of both sexes, that made it clear just how important *both* parents are in the raising of children. And how much harm is done when the man is absent or unwilling to provide the safety, interest, commitment and love that every child needs.

It's true that feminists have also had to show that women can raise children successfully without a father when that is necessary, or when the safety of children would otherwise be at risk. But this in no way diminishes the crucial insight: *fathers matter*. And, good or bad, the effects of their parenting will go on reverberating throughout their children's lifetime.

IN FLOURISHING FAMILIES, parents will aim to work together harmoniously and—significantly—will support one another in their parenting. Each will make the effort to understand and respect what the other one is doing. Neither will undermine their partner through criticizing or trivializing their separate contributions. (So easy to overlook what you never do yourself.)

The phrase "team family" really does have some meaning. A capacity to offer explicit encouragement, gratitude and especially appreciation is truly priceless. But what is also just as interesting is that in those same more cooperative families, while there will be considerable overlap in what each parent does (they both know how to make a meal, monitor health issues, help with homework, play and pick up toys), they will also have roles that are specific and distinct.

WHEN A COUPLE become parents for the first time, it's likely that the new father will best support both the baby and his unfolding sense of himself as a father by giving most of his support to the new mother: anticipating and meeting her needs so that she can meet the inexhaustible needs of her new baby.

This vital support role requires considerable selflessness. (As does every aspect of parenting.) It is precisely when a man can step up and play his different but essential part in parenting, however, that he will set the tone for mutually supportive parenting ahead, as well as for his specific and infinitely rewarding fathering.

As INFANTS become toddlers, then little children, the role that fathers play changes fast. Even with both parents in the workforce, fathers will still often represent the outside world and its values more powerfully than mothers do.

How fathers interpret the outside world and bring it home to their children, through discussions, and especially through example, sharply impacts on the way children see themselves in the social universe. What Dad values and believes, where he gives his time, how he deals with disappointment and conflict, whether he's consistent and reliable, when and how he "takes charge," and particularly how loving and supportive he is to Mom: these are all factors that will have a huge impact on the psychological development of children. They will also have a huge impact on the worldview his children will develop. And on what kind of man Dad himself will become.

OLDER MEN often sincerely regret their peripheral involvement with their own children, especially in the earliest years when work can make such unyielding demands. Nothing matters more for a father than to comprehend *while he is in the thick of it* just how important family life is to him—and he to it. This means putting family life right at the top of his agenda, not in theory only, but in practice. It means making any big decisions in the context of how they will affect family life and support him to become an even better parent. It may mean shifting away from the usual assumptions that raising kids is basically women's business. It will certainly mean regarding parenting as a *shared* joy and responsibility.

What this adds up to for increasing numbers of men is being an active, committed and truly engaged as well as loving parent, living in the heart of family life, not standing at the edge looking in.

What a Wonderful World

When I am giving a guided meditation I often start not with the mind and thoughts but with the feet, inviting those present to notice for a few moments how satisfying it feels to become consciously aware of where the soles of their feet meet the solidity of the floor or earth. (Nice, too, that the bottom of the foot is called a "sole"!) As we deepen that connection simply by noticing it, it is easy to become aware of how dependent we are on the earth, and to experience with gratitude how possible it is to ground and calm ourselves from the feet upward.

Similarly, when I teach creative journal writing, I urge people to consider setting aside their computers and all the writing habits they associate with them and to write in their journals by hand. Picking up a pen, allowing your hand to move across the page, engaging the intricately related activities of brain and hand, may not produce better writing but it can certainly produce freer and more connected writing. In journal writing—one of the most effective forms of self-therapy that exists—this switch can quickly lead to insights the person seldom expects.

• • •

NOTICING HOW effective it is to meditate from the soles up, or how freeing it can be sometimes to write with a pen rather than via a keyboard, I am also aware of how vital it is to spend time in physical activities that connect us with the real rather than the virtual world(s).

I am not talking about exercise now, although that, too, has its well-rehearsed values. No, what I mean is using our bodies, imagination and senses in ways that connect us directly with the elemental world and, simultaneously, with a sense of stability and pleasure within ourselves.

ADULTS INVARIABLY benefit from taking up real-world physical activities. There's no end to what these could be, including crafts of so many kinds, music, dance, gardening (even on a window ledge), cooking, writing, painting, making scrapbooks or collages, messing about in a shed or on a boat.

Children need these activities, I believe, even more vitally. In fact, I would go so far as to say that their need for engaged, physical activity is almost as great as their need for rest, food and water.

Restless, anxious children can't identify or articulate their need for real-world play but it is sobering to observe how even the most agitated child can be soothed through this kind of activity when it is introduced confidently and offered every day.

Observing children, we can see how great their need is to run free; to play in sand; to create a miniature world with sticks and mud; to throw themselves repeatedly into the ocean; to pick flowers, add water and laboriously make "scent" (just as I remember doing);

to dam a small creek; to plant and harvest a fast-growing vegetable crop; to sleep a night under the stars or in a tent; or to run up a small hill and roll all the way down again.

Swimming, running, riding, taking long walks for moment-by-moment discovery and not to get somewhere, listening to and telling stories, singing familiar and new songs, learning rhythmic poetry by heart and chanting it out loud, playing make-believe, or playing and cooperating without comparing or needing particular skills, taking time out simply to lie down, drift and be: this is the best therapy—the best play, the best fun—any child could have.

THE SEDUCTIONS of the virtual worlds are powerful. Children are allured by those enchantments and it can be convenient for parents to respond. Also, time is often short. And many people live without a yard. But this is not an either/or.

The whole world can be a shared garden if we want that. Painting, clay work, collage or block building can be done on a table. The smallest balcony can become a garden. The night sky is a wonder wherever you live. The nearest park can become an extension of home. A bus ride can take you to the edge of a city, or to a new town with new sights and new adventures.

Children long to know and feel part of the wider world. These primal longings can't be satisfied by virtual experiences. They—and we—need firsthand experiences to feel content and complete.

Easy to Like

W e all want people to like our children. We want them to be socially confident. And we want them to know how to consider and cooperate with other people. These are reasonable social goals that will be highly significant in terms of their eventual success and personal happiness. But this will never be possible unless we are prepared to invest the time and small effort needed to ensure that our darlings are capable of being alert, empathic and courteous.

Courtesy is not an old-fashioned virtue. It is a timeless one and central to considering other people. Considering others is the foundation of kindness. This is a basic insight of emotional intelligence. Just as basic is the understanding that people who can be trusted to be thoughtful are delightful to be around, while those who have little idea how to think of others or care about them are difficult and sometimes impossible to be with.

IT SHOULD BE EASY to teach children the basic courtesies that will make them likable and a pleasure to be with. Yet, looking around, it plainly isn't.

Such teaching would include the great invariables of "please" and "thank you." It would also include learning to ask, "And how are you?" when someone asks, "How are you?" Or to inquire, "How was your day?" and listening with interest to the answer. It would include saying, "Excuse me" if you need someone's attention or are passing in front of anyone or, "Can you please wait a moment?" if you need a moment. In most Western contexts it includes being able to make eye contact. And to sustain a little communication beyond the bare necessities.

It would include using people's names to emphasize the connection: "Thank you, Mrs. Rose"; "Please, Mom, may I . . .?"; "Hello, Kim!" It also has to necessitate some basic lessons in self-control, like not interrupting constantly (when you are older than three); not yelling from the other end of the house (because you don't want to leave your chair or computer game); not swearing, abusing or demanding; not screaming like a despot when you don't get your own way.

Knowing how to sit at a table and eat a meal with a knife and fork is also pretty basic. As is making passably interesting conversation with other people while you eat. (It lifts children's confidence mightily when they know how to listen and talk with a variety of people.)

Learning to set the dinner table is as necessary for boys as it is for girls. So are the everyday household tasks of clearing up, stacking and emptying the dishwasher or washing up and drying, bed making, tidying up after your own activities, feeding pets, perhaps bringing in and folding the washing, watering the garden and, quite early on, making or helping to make simple meals.

IT IS A MARK of respect for your children to assume that they *can* learn to be courteous and helpful. This needs to be an unconditional expectation, not something to be hedged or won with bribes and cajoling.

It is of course virtually impossible to teach these everyday civilities as theory only. Your own treatment of friends, the children's teachers and friends, the children themselves and, most consistently of all, your partner, is the most effective teaching tool you have. Rudeness doesn't undermine kindness only; it also erodes trust and intimacy.

Your children deserve to be appreciated and liked by people outside your immediate family. They also deserve to be easy to live with *within* the family. Appreciating these social skills and the values that they express, you are supporting their emotional well-being, poise and relationships throughout a lifetime.

THESE SKILLS will certainly include apologizing meaningfully but with no sense of humiliation when they (or you) have done something wrong (as everyone will from time to time). And in order to keep children safe, *it must include teaching each child that they have the right to say no as well as yes.*

This last point is crucial. Children who are respected as well as loved will innately learn what emotional boundaries are, and what they should mean. They will know when there is any threat, danger or transgression. And they will trust that others can and will listen when they speak up.

This is social education 101. Easy to teach; easy to learn. We can't afford to fail our children. We can't afford to fail ourselves.

"I Only Want Them to Be Happy"

🌀

Other than good health, most parents want nothing more for their children than happiness. Equally, nothing causes them greater pain than their children's sorrows.

Nevertheless, the role played by parents in their children's happiness is not straightforward, especially as babies grow into children and their needs and their parents' responses become more complex. Whenever I am speaking in public about happiness, I am struck by how vulnerable many people feel when it comes to this crucial aspect of their children's well-being. They are clear about their desire for happiness. They are not clear how best to support it. And they are certainly not clear about how best to support their children through times of *un*happiness, only some of which may be the tragedies they first appear.

CHILDREN ARE NOT simply blank slates, waiting to soak up and reflect our favorite theories. Children can also be our teachers. Observe children who are absorbed in something that intrigues or delights them; or open to the awe and wonder of something in the world around them; or eating, laughing, singing or chatting; or painting or building or making something with unself-conscious delight: it is clear that happiness is a truly natural experience. However, the experiences of frustration, disappointment and inner and outer conflict are also natural and inevitable.

Taking this seriously, you will know that it is in showing how much you yourself enjoy the people around you and your activities, *and* how well you deal with those less welcome moments of conflict, disappointment and frustration, that you will best guide and develop your child's inner well-being.

How PARENTS think about happiness already makes a difference. Most people are inclined to associate happiness with pleasure and with things going well. Getting what we want *when we want it* may seem essential to happiness. But that is a very limited view of what happiness is. It may also give moments of "not happiness" more weight and drama than they possibly deserve.

Listening to an older child scream when they don't get what they want is horrible. (It's even more horrible watching an adult screaming out their frustrations or self-pitying accusations, or having a terrible-twos tantrum.) Yet if we don't learn to endure and survive our inevitable frustrations, it becomes extremely difficult to discover that our happiness doesn't depend on everything going our way.

To make any claim to inner peace and resilience, we have to know that, good or bad, every moment will pass. With each new day, the sun will rise again. We also have to know that our needs will sometimes clash with others' needs and that we can and must learn how to compromise and be generous. And that we will sometimes gain a great deal by giving up something small.

As adults we know that it's when our own limited or most immediate appetites or needs rule us that we have most difficulty soothing ourselves and carrying on. The same rule applies to children.

THROUGH EVERYDAY experiences, children learn how rich their
personal, social and physical worlds are. It's also through experience
that they learn how possible it is to survive most times of disappointment and frustration—and get over them. This is where
some judicious coaching can be immensely helpful. Different families will use different phrases, but the emphasis that helps most is
the truest: "This will pass."

It is important not to discount the passion and intensity of children's feelings. But it is just as important not to be fearful of their
feelings or overwhelmed by them. Demonstrating that you can care
and stand back a little, you again give a fine example. With the lit-
tlest children it really is possible often to "kiss things better." Older
children are helped with a simple phrase that looks to the future:

- "I suspect this will feel a good bit better tomorrow."
- "I often find something easier is just around the corner."
- "You can be sure it will feel easier in the morning."
- "Let's think about what else we can look forward to and plan."
- "We are both going to have to put on our thinking caps and
  find a way out of this one."
- "I know you're getting there . . . things will get better."

Your choice of phrase matters far less than its emphasis and positive message, assuring children that they won't be stuck in their
unhappiness: that events will move on and so can they. (And that

you will think *with* them if the situation is a tough one.) A phrase that works for you and your children is hypnotic in its power, and well-supported children will soon learn to use it to soothe themselves when you are not around.

THOSE FIRSTHAND experiences of getting over unhappiness, and moving on, are essential if children are to develop a less fragile as well as less anxious view of themselves. This is helped when they can take in and hold on to (talk about, celebrate, remember) good experiences as well as disappointing ones. And when they can pay attention to what they already have, rather than constantly running ahead to what they don't have.

Parents know how painful it is to be accused of not doing that one more thing, having just done two or ten other things: "You didn't buy me a green army man . . . You never . . . My friend Bessie always . . . Her mom lets her . . ." Hearing that rising whine—and hurt by the injustice of it—it is hard for parents not to feel sorry for themselves. They might also feel mystified as to how they could have raised this unpleasant, thankless child! So perhaps it helps to remember that appreciating what you already have, taking that in and not jumping ahead to focus on the next unfulfilled desire is something countless adults also struggle with. In a competitive, anxious society like ours, the highly subjective experience of "enough" can be tough for children to understand. So it's good to know that, as with so many interactions with our children, this notion of enough, and of setting limits, is also best learned through everyday conversation and example.

How you deal with your own feelings is crucial here. *You need to know when what you have already done or given is enough.* And when what you have is also enough. When you and your partner talk about what's going well and working well, about your feelings of sufficiency and confidence rather than resentment; when you deal with conflict cooperatively; when you successfully negotiate difference: *you give a priceless example to your children*.

PERHAPS THE SIMPLEST lesson to learn in having more family happiness and less unhappiness is also the most effective: *the more dramatic the situation, the calmer we ourselves need to be*. However tempting it is to lose our cool, we don't help our children in any tense situation by getting angry with them or with ourselves. We don't help them, either, by humiliating them, discounting their emotions, or by giving in, "just this once."

Setting limits, knowing when enough truly is enough, feeling confident that every whim does not have to be catered to, demonstrating patience and concern without slipping into tragedy mode, you give your child an invaluable sense of safety. Experience by experience, they will discover that disappointments can be survived and conflicts resolved. They may not like all your decisions. They may not even like all your choices. But at least they will know you are capable of making them.

No Single Recipe
for Resilience

❧

Children have a natural appetite for happiness. To sustain this joy in living and to grow in appreciation for their own lives they can and must learn to bear life's inevitable disappointments and frustrations. Many factors will influence their capacity to do this. A supportive, encouraging atmosphere in the home is critical. The example parents give through their own lives, and how they talk about setbacks or negotiate conflict, is just as important. But any parent with more than one child will also know that our children's capacity for resilience and happiness varies, too, according to their genes and temperament.

Some children bounce back from difficulties far more easily than others. And we know that from the earliest ages some children will brood on every real or perceived hurt. What that means is that no single happiness "recipe" will work easily or simply for every child.

Knowing what particularly arouses your child's anxieties or frustrations, you can help them to discover what best soothes them or helps them to soothe themselves. For example, in the face of an upset, some children will want to talk about how they are feeling right then and there, and *be listened to*. Others may respond better to distraction. Others will want to use the soothing phrases that I referred to in the previous chapter. Or will be grateful to hear you explain briefly and kindly: "When I feel upset, this helps . . ." Many children will want to know how to deal with conflict more effectively but, again, the timing and intensity of this need will vary from child to child.

WHAT UPSETS our children will also vary greatly. Even some very young children may feel enraged about social injustices or the unfairness of adults. Others will care much more about what they perceive as small or great blows to a more fragile sense of self. Some will mind dreadfully about "things"; others will mind far more about friendship hurts, or when the emotional atmosphere at home is unpredictable or in any way frightening. If our child's passions make little sense to us, we need to be particularly careful to show them respect without accelerating the drama.

Every setback is an opportunity to grow in resilience. This is not a quality that can be learned in the abstract. It can only be learned firsthand. Parenting is our chance to learn resilience and go on learning it. Our children's chances to grow in resilience are just as vital.

Perhaps the uppermost element in this resilience picture is that in responding to our children's painful dramas, we need to remain self-aware enough to be calm ourselves. This is frequently a tough test of our self-control and empathy as well as patience. Those qualities are, however, *exactly what we are hoping to develop in them*. In "losing it" we lose more than our temper. We lose a precious chance to demonstrate that we are affected by events, but rarely defeated or discouraged by them.

. . .

As CHILDREN grow older they will discover how much happiness, as well as self-respect and self-confidence, comes their way when they are generally thoughtful, a good friend, and can cooperate successfully with a variety of other people—even with those they don't immediately find easy or like best.

They will notice how rewarding their world is when it includes an awareness of other people in all their variety; when their curiosity is fully fired; when they have passions and interests of their own choosing; when they know themselves to be an integral part of an infinitely wondrous universe.

Those are discoveries that parents will make and renew alongside their children. And that the luckiest children will make alongside their encouraging, resilient parents.

Taking Charge

M ost parents think of the birth of their children as a high point in their lives. But the majority would also admit that turning themselves into relaxed, confident parents remains one of their greatest challenges.

Where I live in a pretty, inner-city neighborhood there's been a rapid increase in the number of babies and little children in recent years. Because I've loved being a parent myself, I find this delightful. Yet, as I watch new parents and listen to those I know personally, I see that a couple of critical cornerstones of parenting are becoming harder to apply. I don't think this is because they are any less useful but rather that they are somewhat out of step with how parents increasingly think about themselves in their nonparenting roles.

The first of these is establishing simple, predictable routines. I don't mean by this that tiny babies should be pushed into a rigid schedule of feeding and sleep. In fact, I feel that's brutal and often damaging. But by the time the child (and parents) emerges from the cocoon of infancy into toddlerhood and beyond, it is incredibly helpful to the parents, and soothing and stabilizing for the child, to have predictable rhythms to most days' and nights' events.

.   .   .

THIS MIGHT at first seem too hard for busy parents to achieve. It doesn't easily fit with work schedules, nor with the increasing need parents have for their children to be flexible. This is where generational needs can so easily clash. Parents may want their children to be able to stay up late some nights but not others, to snatch a rest in the car rather than in bed, and to eat meals late if that's when the adults are ready.

It is understandable parents would value that kind of flexibility. It's how we tend to live our adult lives, hurtling from one thing to another, multitasking madly and responding to what's most urgent rather than what is most important. But while some children will adapt to this, many can't. Tired, irritable or confused children leave even the most loving parents feeling edgy and helpless, creating a situation that can deplete everyone.

The younger a child is, the more they need a soothing rhythm to their days and nights. And the greater the benefits will soon be for the whole family. This includes lots of time for explorative play and exercise, simple meals, eating dinner by 5:30 or 6:00 p.m., early story and bed and a long night's sleep. Even teenagers will usually benefit from eating earlier and sleeping longer. In fact, at whatever age a child is cranky, demanding or "impossible," it's those routines and rhythms that need attention, however inconvenient or impossible that might at first seem.

Parents might also want their children to tolerate intense attention at some times and little or no attention at others, without offering the skills and means for independent play. (Having a small backpack always ready for an outing with a changing range

of toys geared for play away from home is a lifesaver often missing
even in well-off families.)

When planning to be out and about with your children, it's worth
taking a moment to think about how children will interact with a
particular environment, whether it will cause them to feel settled or
fractious, and to plan accordingly. Some adults are easy for children
to be around; some are not. Minimizing the time spent in supermarkets, shopping malls and large department stores, or on public
transport, or anywhere public at all in the rush hour, saves children
and parents alike from predictable stress. It also creates far more
time to discover new delights in friendlier environments.

CREATING RHYTHMS AND ROUTINES, and sensibly anticipating
which environments will be most rewarding and joyful for children,
are choices that only parents can make. Children can't make those
choices for themselves and it is unfair and unhelpful to ask them to
do so.

Choice is the second of those parenting cornerstones in need of
a renaissance, especially a new clarity about which choices the parents can and must make, and when they should avoid bombarding
their children with choices or requiring them to make choices that
are too abstract, confusing or unnecessary.

"Tell me what you feel like" is a request made with the best of
intentions. But it is doubly unhelpful. First, you don't want your
child constantly to be scrutinizing their feelings rather than simply
getting on with things. Second, and as critically, none of us benefits when we do things only because we "feel like it" rather than
because it needs to or can be done. In fact, doing things because
we feel like it (or otherwise not), we become slaves to our feelings,

rather than knowing we can cooperate with them and that they can support rather than limit us.

Although usually done with the best of intentions, the "too-many-choices syndrome" almost always creates tension rather than the desired independence. Cheerfully and confidently stating that it's time to get dressed, eat breakfast, have a walk, go to playgroup or school, have a bath, dinner or a story, or go to bed is realistic. And, echoing the rhythms to the day, it is also deeply reassuring.

The vast majority of children will still have countless opportunities to develop and express their preferences. It's lovely for them to choose the book for their evening story; to wear green shorts with their pink T-shirt; to say clearly that they want to visit Granny or "go home now." But they will make those preferences known far less anxiously and perhaps less insistently when their routines are presented not as a relay of vexing choices, but rather as different experiences within a full and replenishing day.

Emotional Literacy

In every life, learning to read is an achievement. Just as crucial is learning to read our own and other people's emotional messages and signals—and responding skillfully. This is key to successful, considerate relationships. And it is at least as crucial for our wholehearted participation in life as reading any text.

What I am raising is a version of "emotional literacy" and I'm quite convinced that we pay it far less attention than we could or should. Perhaps we expect it to be entirely natural that we would know how to read each other's needs and intentions; that we would be capable of watching someone's expression and learning from it; or observing their body language, taking note and adjusting our own responses.

We may even be assuming that this is particularly easy for parents in relation to their own children. Yet, quite plainly, this is not always the case.

SOME WEEKS AGO I sat near the front of a bus taking me into the city, a journey of about fifteen minutes. During that time, a well-meaning young mother emptied an entire glass jar of baby food into her plump year-old son, despite his eloquent protests. He pursed his lips, screwed up his nose, shook his head, whimpered, turned his head away—and each time he opened his mouth to protest more loudly, she put the spoon in.

As though that was not enough, the mother talked at him constantly, telling him how tasty the food was and how much he was enjoying it. (That unbroken stream of words was almost worse than the food she was pushing into him.) Her reality totally obliterated his. In fact, his "loud and clear" signals remained illegible to her.

I am assuming that this is not because she is a bad mother. She is probably devoted to her son yet she could neither "read" nor interpret his needs as in any way distinct from her own agenda.

THIS WAS such a tiny incident. It has real consequences, however. As this tiny boy learns that his signals mean so little to his mother, he will also learn to distrust his own inner signals and particularly his instincts around food, emotions and connections of many kinds. His capacity to read himself inwardly will be suppressed or become confusing. And what is so sad is how routine such situations are in countless good people's lives, even when spoken language becomes available. *I feel this; you tell me I feel that.*

To TAKE emotional literacy seriously, we must learn first how to get out of the way of our own wishes and inner commentaries. We need to do this *before* we can begin to read the reality that's unfolding before our eyes.

We need to be more than caring, in fact. At the very least, we "open our eyes"—and minds—when we are curious and investigative in our thinking, when we can happily accept that there's always more to know, when we are capable of learning from our interactions with other people, and of changing our minds and expectations.

THERE ARE TIMES when adults' greater knowledge and experience must prevail—especially when it comes to keeping children safe, clean, protected, and so on. But this won't be more successfully achieved by insisting that your child has no right to their separate needs, appetites, interests and existence.

The plump, delightful baby I saw on the bus wasn't starving. And the mother did not increase her son's appetite by insisting that he was hungry and was enjoying his food when, so plainly, he was not. Out of blindness to anything but her own interpretations and agenda, this caring mother pushed spoon after spoon of food into him, while also denying him confidence in his needs—and in his vital power to communicate those needs.

This is such a memorable example of how intimacy depends on *self*-awareness, as well as awareness of others. It also shows how much humility as well as love is needed as we learn and relearn how to be the parents our children need.

Character Building

✿

Parents want their children to be resilient. They want them to be liked and likable. They want them to be cooperative, caring, playful and affectionate. They want them to be honest, trustworthy and ethical. But how should this be achieved?

How can children be taught to meet their inevitable setbacks with relative calm? Or to perceive their fears as something normal that they can recover and even learn from? How can they learn to see situations from someone else's point of view? Or get enough sense of proportion that every molehill doesn't have to be a mountain?

What will help them notice that they must sometimes take their turn, rather than believing that their agenda must always be paramount? How will they (eventually) learn to take responsibility for their mistakes, rather than blaming and raging at someone else?

How will they learn the saving graces of thoughtfulness and kindness? And know how possible it is to be kind even when this doesn't get you what you want? And, as crucially, how will parents learn to trust their child's resilience and strengths, rather than protecting them from any real or perceived fragilities?

. . .

THESE ARE CHALLENGES that lots of parents find difficult to face. Yet thinking about how we regard life, and what we believe will best support us *through* life, is at least as essential as any other aspect of parenting.

Some families believe that it is the job of a school, church, temple or community to give the moral guidance and ethical insights that character building demands. I disagree. Parents are their children's first and most influential teachers. In the intimacy and constancy of home, children will always pick up on how their parents see themselves, what they believe in, and what they regard as most important.

In a fortunate home, there will be space to try out new ideas without being told you are wrong. There will be space for everyone to talk—and a willingness to listen. There will be an exploration of some of the big ethical issues of the day. And, most crucially, the values the parents espouse will match how they live.

Children are highly sensitive to issues of injustice and hypocrisy. There's no point in Dad yelling at his young son to control his temper or stop being rude to his mother if Dad himself is bad-tempered, rude or both. There is no point in Mom urging her children to be generous or forgiving if she herself is complaining about how grim or unfair life is. There is no use pushing your children to make an effort with their studies if they never see you read a book or discuss a serious issue. In religious families, particularly, it is unbearable for children to be expected to be loving and good if their parents are argumentative, critical, unloving or unkind.

Noticing how necessary it is that we "walk the talk" (or keep silent), we gain a precious chance to lift our own game. *Noticing* what qualities and values we most wish our children to develop, we can and must develop them more consciously in ourselves.

Believing in your child's capacity to develop strengths as well as values is essential. So is demonstrating how your own values support, guide and keep you more secure. This doesn't mean that you must suddenly become impossibly perfect. In fact, the contrary is true. Recovering from setbacks and disappointments, you help your children. Regretting your failings, you help your children. Resolving to do better—and *doing better*—you help your children. Demonstrating a hopeful resolve and the capacity to move ahead, you help your children. Engaging with the world beyond your own immediate interests, you help your children.

You also help yourself.

Different and the Same

※

There's a funny paradox in the fact that we all value the uniqueness of our children, yet can be slow to help them develop positive attitudes around difference.

Two recent stories from mothers of young children have prompted me to think about these crucial issues. I have been reminded yet again how vital it is that we guide our children to recognize their precious power to be kind. And to understand what a difference this makes for them as well as others. This is what teaches them to be empathic. It is also what will make them inwardly strong, self-respecting and secure.

THE FIRST MOTHER has a little girl, Tessa, who is six. Lively, sweet Tessa has cerebral palsy. It makes walking and talking a constant challenge. Tessa is still enthusiastic about attending her local school. However, what is becoming increasingly obvious to Tessa, and is agonizingly clear to her parents, is that Tessa is being socially sidelined.

When the children are invited to form pairs, Tessa has to be assigned to a not-always-willing partner. When the girls huddle in groups at lunchtime, no one reaches out to Tessa. When party invitations are distributed, Tessa rarely gets one. Her mother said to me, as angry as she was hurt, "We invited all the girls and several boys to a wonderful party when Tessa turned six. Their parents were in our home. They can see how sociable Tessa is and that her friendship needs are exactly the same as for their girls. Yet not one of those parents has guided their children or insisted that they invite Tessa back."

The second story is less painful but no less challenging. This time it was the mother of eight-year-old Jacob who was wondering what I thought her son's rights were to refuse invitations from classmates when he was asked to parties and didn't want to go.

In his class, the custom is to ask all the children of the same sex. (Perhaps a similar custom would help Tessa.) Problems come for Jacob when the promised party games are far rougher than he is comfortable with. But does he have the right to refuse an invitation? Should his parents insist he learn to confront uncomfortable situations without being intimidated by them?

EACH OF THESE STORIES, it seems to me, is more about the parents than the children. In situations like Tessa's—and they abound in our schools—it's the adults who already know how devastating it is to be shut out on the basis of difference. And in my view it is up to the adults to do something about it.

Six-year-old children *are* capable of empathy. Yet girls and boys of this age are also, inevitably, highly self-focused. To help them to take into account the feelings of a vulnerable little girl, they need guidance.

It is a horrible lesson to learn that you can or even "should" exclude people on the basis of difference. In contrast, it is a wonder-ful lesson to learn that although some people are more obviously "different," *in reality we all have our differences.* Some are simply less obvious than others.

Children can also readily comprehend that in wanting friendship and acceptance—including invitations to parties and someone to sit with at lunchtime—*we are very much the same.*

These are lessons we may need to learn repeatedly. They are vital for compassionate, empathic living. They are also vital for self-confidence and self-respect.

Excluding any child on the basis of difference makes *all* the chil-dren more vulnerable and self-defensive. ("When is it my turn to be left out?") Parents can't make their children become friends with Tessa. What they can do is strictly censor any laughter or mean comments at Tessa's expense. They can point to her particular chal-lenges without making her an object of pity. They can and should influence a friendly attitude, mainly by minimizing those physical differences and pointing out emotional and social similarities.

Most crucially, those parents can model through their own atti-tudes and ease with difference that genuine inclusion is "how we do things around here." The value of that lesson will go way beyond the six-year-old class setting.

And for Jacob's parents?

The choice to say no also has lifelong implications. If Jacob is routinely avoiding social situations, then he will need active encour-agement to be a little braver. One of the greatest opportunities that school offers is the chance to enlarge your social world through new friends and experiences. On the other hand, if he is already reasonably comfortable with other children and it is only potentially aggressive play that Jacob wants to avoid (or watching scary movies or playing violent computer games), then I believe he is entitled to assert his wishes and stay at home.

Once again, how the parents guide this situation is crucial. They can support Jacob to say no, quietly, to the party invitation, without making any kind of elaborate moral judgment of the other child or his family.

Learning that you can say no as well as yes is crucial for children. Learning how empowering it is to look beyond superficial differences to what we share is just as vital.

Family Explosions

❊

Our emotional well-being depends to a great extent on how fairly and kindly other people treat us. (How we treat others affects *their* well-being just as directly.) But where does that leave us when we are unsure what to expect of others? Or unsure whether our demands are halfway reasonable? This is an issue that affects countless households, often in a repetitive and frustrating way.

Here's an all-too-familiar example. Mom feels overstretched and unappreciated. It's background noise to her emotional life and part of the reason she feels so tired. Arriving home after a day at work and a lengthy detour to the supermarket, she asks Henry, her oldest child, for help bringing in the shopping from the car. Henry's fourteen and is busy texting.

He asks Mom to hang on a minute. And Mom loses it. She explodes with irritation, disappointment and anger—not because of that delay, but because for her it typifies so many moments when she needs help and doesn't get it. Or when her needs are entirely ignored by the people she loves most.

But what happens next? Henry looks up from his phone and is outraged that the mad harridan in front of him is yelling. About what? About him not "jumping to"? Is that what she's going on about? Now it's his turn to be self-righteous. Does she see him as a lackey to jump to her every command and salute while doing so?

Henry also feels devalued. And hopping mad.

IT WOULD BE entirely possible to write a comedy series about domestic moments as simultaneously trivial and momentous as this one. Yet the living of them is rarely funny. Messages get mixed. Family communication and goodwill collapses. The truly important is not expressed. What should be unimportant becomes Wagnerian.

MISUNDERSTANDINGS may be inevitable in families. Emotions are always close to the surface, and they run very deep. This makes it more and not less vital that when miscommunications happen often, or are badly handled, they should be taken seriously. Whatever the "cause" or catalyst, their effects will hurt.

In this situation, for example, what happens when Dad or one of the other children comes home and each person wants their version of the story to be heard and validated? Taking sides may make one person feel momentarily better, yet it leaves the other person stranded. It solves nothing and may make the situation worse.

In fortunate families, a sense of proportion will soon reassert itself. One person will apologize and explain how difficult or exhausting their day was. The other person will acknowledge their matching overreaction. A quick hug, and life continues.

But even when things do calm down relatively fast, it is worth taking time to think hard about the assumptions that each person is making, what resentments they are brooding on, and how their needs are being expressed as well as met.

. . .

PROBLEMS CAN escalate fast when we forget that no one can read our thoughts. And we can't read our loved ones' thoughts either! So often our hurt is about what people have failed to do when *they had no idea that was what we wanted.* Or when we assume we know what someone is thinking when, in fact, those thoughts *exist only in our own imagination.*

Intimate situations—and what situation is more intimate than family life?—are hotbeds of misunderstanding and projections (assuming someone else is thinking what you yourself fear; responding to your partner as if she is your mother; venting your frustration with your own insecurities at your most insecure child . . .). This is what makes the rules of clear, respectful communication not just essential but lifesaving.

In this particular scenario, the weary mother did indeed ask her son for help, but he couldn't possibly have known—particularly in the midst of texting—why her request was so urgent or how starved she was more generally for consideration and support.

Equally, when Henry asked his mom to wait a minute, that was literally what he meant. But she heard, "Your needs can wait." Perhaps she even heard, "Your needs don't matter." Or, worse yet, "*You* don't matter." And in the noise of his mother's frustrated explosion Henry heard, "Never mind your text or your agenda. Only *my* agenda matters."

IT IS NEVER EASY to assess whether our most outraged reactions have been justified. And perhaps that's not what matters most.

Whenever there are outbreaks of hurt and misunderstanding, communications need to be clearer, more respectful and direct.

Three simple insights might help.

Because most explosions of this kind happen when people are tired, hungry or overwhelmed, or have *not* been expressing their needs clearly, never try to sort out the fairness of the situation while you are caught up in the heat of the moment. *Take a significant break.*

When you are ready, *look at the situation coolly from the other person's point of view.* You can also check out the validity of your assumptions. ("I thought you were saying . . . Was that what you meant?") Seeing how differently each person heard and understood the situation can take the sting out of it.

Finally, *consider how and whether you are making your needs clear.* You may be reluctant to ask for help or to receive it. Or to say honestly how you are feeling. Yet this is always preferable to mutual second-guessing, or acting out your rage or disappointments—and living with the consequences.

Pet Food

✦

As every pet lover knows, pets are exceptionally enlightened teachers. Our beloved family cats are getting old now, although one of them, at least, is clearly going to go to the grave believing he is still a kitten. This is a phenomenon enchanting in cats, and perhaps less so in other species. However, it is not the eternal youth of Younger Cat that has been intriguing me but that both of them, in different ways, have been having increasing trouble with what my grandmother might have called their "waterworks." Again, that's not something unique to felines, but where it becomes more interesting is that we've had to discover that there are very specific dietary recommendations for elderly dogs as well as cats with renal or urinary tract weaknesses.

Without going into the science of these diets, which would bore you and be beyond me, it's further evidence that some foods will aid the body's functions and other foods will diminish it. And unless our pets are even cleverer than we assume and are quietly reading the small print on labels, this clearly isn't a case of mind over matter.

. . .

DIFFERENT FOODS affect pets' bodies differently. What's more, when their physical health improves, so do their sleep, energy, mood, playfulness and joy in living. *And we human beings are no different.* What we eat, as well as how and when we eat, affects us physiologically and emotionally. Yet we are often immensely reluctant to take this seriously.

Thanks to the media's obsession with food, diets, body shapes and weight, we are literally stuffed with advice and information about which foods are good for us and which harm us. Perennial stomach pains, digestive problems, poor sleep, blood sugar spikes, headaches, breathing difficulties, high blood pressure, worrying cholesterol levels, overweight or underweight and lack of energy and vibrancy are just some reasons to suggest that we need to pay closer attention to what food and drinks we are routinely choosing.

DOING THAT, our minds will inevitably turn toward our common eating sins. And I must confess I find it hard to be patient when thinking about parents who would ignore the avalanche of contemporary information and continue to find reasons to give their children food that makes them hysterical or starves them of essential nutrients for the brain as well as their bones. Artificial sweeteners, colors that shriek "chemicals," sugar-laden cookies and cakes, foods laden in fats, and prepackaged food all affect brain function and mood. Worse, they make our children fat, flabby and far weaker than they should be.

. . .

GIVING IN TO children's demands for junk is a betrayal not just of their health but also of our common sense. Children are not able to think ahead in the ways that adults can and should. Immediate gratification is what rules kids' minds, which is why they have an excuse for the occasional tantrum or meltdown but we don't. When it comes to food, *we must think for them*. And we must set the best possible example by eating well ourselves. And relishing doing so.

BUYING AND PREPARING food is one of the areas of life that is easiest for us to control. Money is not even the crucial issue here because with the smallest space on a balcony it is possible to grow some greens or herbs. And on the smallest budget it is still possible to eat delicious fresh food that changes not just with the seasons but also, in varying combinations, on a daily basis.

All of which raises fascinating questions about why so many of us remain stubbornly blind to the evidence before our eyes, as well as why we would refuse to take responsibility for our health and lives more generally.

The usual culprits loom large here: habit, perhaps laziness, and certainly that familiar unwillingness to sacrifice immediate pleasures for lifelong gains. Sometimes we have allowed our children to become addicted to sugar and fat "hits," and will need to make healthy food even more appealing to wean them (and ourselves) away from that.

A surprising number of people also struggle with a sense of disconnection from their bodies, ignoring the signals their bodies are constantly sending. Those people may well spend lots of time obsessing about how they are feeling or how they look without making the leap to taking charge of their food, health and life.

A serious illness can provide an urgent wake-up call. So can significant obesity or an eating disorder in our children or ourselves. (Starving the body can be even more dangerous than feeding it rubbish.) But how sad it is that a crisis of that magnitude is so often required before people are driven to find more supportive, kinder solutions.

The most powerful person in your life when it comes to health is your own self. The most powerful people in children's lives when it comes to food are their parents. It's almost embarrassing to write that fresh food can make a phenomenal difference in keeping them and us well. And that even in the most pessimistic household it takes a surprisingly short time to abandon old habits and shore up new ones. What's even better is that making positive, self-supporting choices about what's going into your mouth and building your body can give you a renewed sense of power in your life (and your parenting) more broadly.

WHEN IT COMES TO FOOD, the "rules" couldn't be easier. Fresh, varied, colorful and minimally processed is the way to go. The fresher and more "alive" your food, the more alive you will feel eating it. No recipe could be simpler. Or more fail-safe.

Personally Responsible

٭

Teaching children that they can be responsible for their choices and for their behavior is one of the biggest challenges of parenting. It can make even the early days of never knowing when the baby will sleep or settle down seem like a benign dream.

Rules are tricky but it is widely accepted that parents of younger children should remain confidently in charge of the big decisions while gradually handing over appropriate responsibility for small daily tasks and also (and more crucially) for the *effects of their children's choices and behavior.* This gradually develops the insights that all children need as they make their way toward a self-determining and self-respectful adulthood.

The vision a few years ago of the celebrity Paris Hilton, then twenty-six, crying out to her mother that the judge's decision in her drunk-driving case to return her to jail was "not fair," told us more than we needed to know about how poorly a sense of responsibility was nurtured *chez* Hilton. But many parents will have some sneaking sympathy, at least with Paris's parents, because guiding others to be genuinely self-responsible is an art—requiring much higher levels of consistency and care from the parents than from the children.

. . .

WHEN MY OWN CHILDREN were young I read a book called *Liberated Parents, Liberated Children*, by Adele Faber and Elaine Mazlish, that suggested the best way to teach children how to be responsible was to give up "rescuing" them. For example, your child refuses to get dressed in time for school? You take him to school in his pajamas. Your child fails to feed her goldfish or rabbit and you don't take over even when rigor mortis is about to set in. Your child refuses to eat a perfectly acceptable dinner so you clear the table and don't cook anything else. Your child fails to write out her birthday invitations. You don't nag. And you don't write them for her. Your boys spend all their pocket money at the beginning of the week. You don't compensate even when this means going without something needed. Your older child's homework assignment is late. You don't do their research—or the writing up of it—for them.

The principle is terrific. It's packed with merit. But it's far easier said than done.

Looking back, I know that I was never willing to shame my children, even to develop these priceless gifts. I also hated them to get into trouble. I probably did rescue them more often than was needed, perhaps because I underestimated my own resilience as well as theirs. Where I did do better was in trying to choose the middle way: letting them know that I would support and defend them whenever possible but also that *their* choices, attitudes and actions truly did have consequences.

STANDING BACK FROM doing things for children that they could easily be doing for themselves is also crucial to the not-rescuing picture. It is tempting to tell yourself that it's deeply caring to cut up food for your six-year-old or clean up your ten-year-old's messes. It's just as tempting to make excuses to her teachers for your sullen sixteen-year-old. But it's not caring. And it's not helpful.

"Doing everything" for those you love can be an expression of anxiety (yours, not theirs!). It is also a form of control. By contrast, giving responsibility to your children—even when things might and will sometimes go wrong—expresses trust. It also teaches cooperation and how crucially cooperation is needed in all situations, especially within families.

None of this is best achieved with excessive praise, either. (Nor indifference.) Indiscriminate praise is one of the hallmarks of contemporary parenting. But after the age of two or three, it dilutes the power of what you are saying. It makes praise itself meaningless. Giving responsibilities to children that are manageable and appropriate, you don't then need to act astounded each time they meet those goals. Judicious descriptive praise works best. Or a simple thank-you. This means noticing something that is done well and being specific about it ("I like the way you have rearranged your shelves. Does it make it easier to find your things?"). It also means biting your tongue when they do something differently from the way that you would. That's their business, not yours.

CHILDREN FLOURISH when they are trusted. They also benefit—and are likely to need less nagging—when you take it for granted that they *are* capable. You don't need them to be perfect. They don't need you to be harsh. Noticing what they can contribute, and the fairness of it, they will see themselves positively. They will also see that what they are doing benefits everyone in their small, precious world. And they will take their own measure from that.

Patience Is a Virtue

Patience is a virtue,
Possess it if you can.
Seldom found in woman,
Never found in man.

Standing in my local supermarket recently, somewhere between rice that takes one minute to "cook" and entire meals that can be served in less than five, I found myself thinking somewhat wistfully about the quality of patience and especially about what a vast difference it makes when we are prepared to value and cultivate it.

Some lovely people are naturally patient. And some cultures value patience. They make it easier to learn, too, by overtly disapproving any failures and curbing people's "right" to spit out their frustrations on everyone around them.

Patient people are delightful to be around. They have an innate sense of perspective, not confusing small setbacks or frustrations with large. They don't overvalue their time or act as if time's being stolen from them when things take longer than they hoped. They are also willing to try things more than once without any sense of frustration or failure. And to let other people move forward at their own pace, and do things in their own way.

There's serenity to a patient person that's deeply attractive. And a sense, too, that they are living from the deeper reaches of life, rather than twirling on the surface.

THOSE WITH less patience seem, even from early childhood, to be easily frustrated and overwhelmed, quick to flare, snap or snarl when things take too long or don't go their way. Stuck in a line or a traffic jam, asked to wait an hour for dinner or to redo a task at work; listening to someone retell a familiar story or watching someone tackle something cautiously or clumsily or just differently from the way that they would: all of this can seem like a personal affront to the chronically impatient.

Their worst outbursts may be directed against themselves. But they often take their difficulties out on everyone around them, including their own children.

LOOKING AROUND, not least in supermarkets, I can see that many children suffer deeply from the impatience of their parents and quite obviously hate and fear the irritability and outbursts that go with it.

Impatience is not an excuse for bad or sour moods; it's a cause. We may blame the situation for our own lack of control but to do that is to look entirely in the wrong direction. Self-mastery is needed, and a greater sense of inner spaciousness and even confidence. But we discover that in the moments that impatience flares or threatens, not before. *Whatever inconveniences or most frustrates us can teach us patience.* In fact, it is only the challenging moments in life that are uncomfortable enough to teach us this timeless virtue. This is no small thing: to turn an uncomfortable or *affronting* moment into spacious gratitude for what we are learning and even who we are!

Many of these moments will occur in the company of children. Their energy, the constancy of their demands, their legitimate needs will unfailingly show us how small our allowance of patience really is. Any relationship significant enough to challenge our egocentricity requires endless patience—but none more so than those with our own or others' children. And yet isn't it true that we can and will do for them what we are often unable to do for any other reason? They *are* our reason, not least because we love them and can see what our lack of patience costs them.

Like all the timeless virtues, patience has to be learned through the living of it. No one can make us more patient. We have to see patience's benefits and want them for ourselves. We have to take patience as a vital expression of kindness, take it on as a way of living, take it on as a challenge, sometimes on a daily or even hourly basis.

WHEN MY CHILDREN were very young I used to walk with them at the pace of a snail around the streets or into the park near our home. I was in my middle thirties and had spent many years in the workforce before my first child was born. I was used to being in highly charged, stimulating environments. It was a huge and hard adjustment to slow down to the walking and gazing pace of a one-year-old, with my second baby in the carriage.

I was forced to question my ideas about achievement and what could or should get completed in a day. I had to revalue the small along with the so-called "big." I was continuing with my writing and doing other paid work, but I had to give up all my familiar ideas about time and how it (and I) should be used. Following the children's pace and needs, rather than insisting on my own, was my first great lesson in mindfulness as well as patience.

AWARENESS OF the present moment is integral to patience. This means letting go of your insistence on how things ought to be (but are not). It means refusing to be filled to the point of eruption by anxiety or frustration about what is *not* happening. It means taking time, rather than being ruled by time. It means opening to meet the present moment exactly as a child does. It means relaxing into the space that you and your children occupy. It may even mean filling that space with simple happiness—and finding that you are already patient enough to do so.

Meditation and Children

M editation is widely praised for its physical and psychological benefits as well as for spiritual well-being. As it becomes more popular, I have noticed an increasing interest also in teaching children to meditate.

This is easier than some might think and the benefits for children as well as their teachers and parents are significant. Children need moments of stillness at least as much as adults do. They need the self-assurance this gives. And they need the respite from too much activity and stimulation outside themselves. Meditation can be like a glass of cool water on a hot day. It needn't take long. But its effects are long lasting.

Even a simple experience of "going inside and being still" will affirm for children that they can soothe, calm and settle themselves. This is a lifetime gift to discover and, given how anxious so many children are, it can also be lifesaving.

As they get older, children can be guided gently to "watch" their thoughts and begin also to see how the mind works. Doing this, they will discover that they can observe how thoughts rise, fall and pass. They can also enjoy and trust this present moment without hurtling through it to the next thing. All of this profoundly helps a child to feel real and safe inside. It helps with that vital developing sense of "I." It helps with creativity, inner stability. And also and quite wonderfully it offers an unmistakable glimpse of connection to life beyond themselves. ("The air I breathe out . . . is the air you breathe in. . . .")

MOST LITTLE CHILDREN can be "in the moment" without any instruction. Whether it is building, drawing, playing make-believe games, creating sand castles or squatting on the ground watching entranced as a lizard slides by, being fully present will seem easy and entirely natural to them. But because we live in such an externally focused society, where being busy frequently depends upon being entertained, and where children may be overstimulated by noise, screens and images, many children don't fully develop their natural inner gifts of awareness, focus and engagement.

Meditation can offer some of those gifts, as well as the priceless experience that it is possible to feel inwardly steady, even when things are not outwardly going well.

WHEN CHILDREN are given the chance to be quiet and still in a group, or at home with you, they will also magically discover how thoughts create atmosphere—and how that atmosphere changes when people are sitting together simply and peacefully *being*.

The way the room settles on the "outside" reflects the way the children are feeling and can settle on the "inside."

Understanding that, or better still just experiencing it, is of tremendous value in learning how powerfully we affect one another through what we think as well as through how we behave.

A BASIC MEDITATION instruction might go something like this: "Let's take a few minutes to see what's happening on the inside rather than the outside. We are going to sit still like mountains . . . as solid and as steady as a mountain is . . . then close our eyes . . . and notice how quiet our breath is as it comes in and out of our nostrils. Let's just notice our breath, in and out softly. . . . As we do that we are going to let everything inside become quieter and softer. . . . Let's notice that. . . . It's so peaceful to feel quiet inside. . . . We are going to stay for a little while in the quiet place that's inside us. . . . Just being there, softly and quietly . . . and we are going to let that quietness go all the way through us and around us, wherever it wants to be."

Having said something like that (slowly!), it is crucial to extend the experience of silence for a few minutes, letting the children enjoy *being*, before saying, gently: "It's time now to notice any noises outside . . . to let them in a little more . . . and to notice how the air feels on our faces and hands . . . and that we are still sitting like a mountain but now we are opening our eyes and moving back into our day . . . stretching our arms and legs if we feel like that . . . and still noticing how lovely that steadiness and stillness are inside ourselves. . . ."

Noticing is part of mindfulness. *Noticing* can also itself be inwardly steadying. A few giggles on the way won't matter, and they will pass surprisingly quickly. Meditation isn't pious. And it need not be solemn, either. Once children have practiced this a few times, it is possible to simply say, ideally once or twice a day, "Let's spend a few moments now in that special quiet place inside ourselves. Let's take a moment to sit like a mountain, breathe as slowly as we would like to, and feel peaceful and strong inside."

For children and adults alike, sitting quietly upright and steady "like a mountain," with hands relaxed, is a powerful signal to the mind that it is time to be centered and peaceful.

FOR CHILDREN who are anxious, physically ill or distressed, and especially those who find it hard to settle, it is of tremendous benefit to include simple healing visualizations.

One example would be for children to surround themselves with golden light, softer than sunlight but just as warming. They can direct the light to wherever it's needed. Or they can simply sit inside it as the light creates a beautiful arc or circle all around them. Inside that cone of light, it is also easy to add on a gentle instruction to "Breathe in kindness, breathe out kindness," or any other quality of their choosing ("Breathe in happy times. . . .").

It is also easy to direct children gently to use their mind's eye (their imagination) to see themselves in a place where they feel particularly safe and trusting, perhaps accompanied by a loving figure who represents safety and support to them. ("Think of the kindest, safest person you know of, and let yourself imagine that person is as near to you now as you want them to be. . . .")

It's good to encourage some positive details here to deepen the visualization: "What is the person wearing today? Are they standing nearby or far away? Are they smiling now? Are you smiling . . . ? And do you have something to say to them . . . or do they have something to say to you? How nice that you can take all the time in the world. Soak up the feelings you get from being in this lovely place, and only when you are ready, bring back those feelings inside your heart. . . . You might also want to bring back a special word to write on a card. Take a moment to see if there is a special word this wise person wants to give you, for you to think about. It could be 'happy,' or 'brave,' or 'gentle' . . . or something I haven't thought of but that you know you need. Take your time. No hurry. Just when you are ready . . . and when you have had enough you can open your eyes!"

Accept *without question* anything the child brings back. And remember that this is a time for them in their imagination; *you are simply their companion*. Neither praise nor disparage anything they have "seen" or "heard," just accept it. Your remarks are most helpful when they are neutral and more general: "Our minds are often surprising. . . . I feel more peaceful myself whatever word I find. . . . Isn't it good to know that our own mind can make us feel so much better?"

IN A MORE EXPLICITLY spiritual setting children can also learn to be a "lighthouse" of good wishes, sending good wishes to wherever they are needed. They can also send good wishes or prayers to any situation or concern in their own lives. Some may like to imagine sitting still in the loving presence of Jesus, or of the Buddha, or their guardian angel, feeling the atmosphere of loving acceptance and safety all around them, inside and out. "Surrounding ourselves with golden light" is a sublime instruction and a beautiful, subtle testimony to the power of the mind to support us rather than cause us worry or grief.

. . .

CHILDREN WILL GAIN immeasurably from discovering they can at least sometimes observe their thoughts rather than feeling pushed around by them. They will also benefit from knowing that at any time, and under virtually any circumstances, they can take a few centering seconds to sit steady like a mountain and *be*. And get up, refreshed.

MOODS

Mood Change

Fit for Life?

Always Powerful

Hungry Minds

The Moody Brain

Good Mood Food

Too Tired to Care

Pleasure and Play

Last Call

Tipping Points

Mood Change

Moods are strange things (and they interest me greatly). Driven as much by thought and interpretations as emotion, and by biology as well as psychology, they can easily feel more powerful than we are. They come. They lift our spirits or lower them. And they go again as a different mood or emotional response takes their place.

Some lucky people are genuinely stable in their moods. If pushed too far, they may become briefly ratty, sharp or anxious. If faced with something serious or sad, their emotions will reflect that. But more generally they are the people who feel pretty positive about life and are unafraid to express that. As significantly, everyone around them can also rely on them being positive and good-humored.

That kind of emotional stability is a gift to be treasured and applauded because so many people have a default mood or emotional stance that's considerably less sunny. I'm not talking about people who are clinically depressed, necessarily. Nor are they suffering from the erratic and painful mood swings that always signal a need for professional assessment and support.

No, today, as I write this, I'm thinking about the people who live life with an inner flatness and absence of pleasure, or a sense of grievance that's constantly finding a new target, or a low-grade irritability that significantly colors how they see the world and everyone around them.

MANY PEOPLE come to view this kind of damped-down existence as normal. And in a way they are right. *It is normal for them*, and the energy it takes to think about change can feel far out of reach. Yet change is needed, in part because a low mood can always slip lower, and also because the person living this relatively bleak, sunless existence is never doing so alone.

Moods are highly contagious. We step into a room and can intuit at once if someone is feeling down. They don't need to talk. Moods "leak" into the atmosphere and, for better or worse, affect everyone.

In the past few weeks alone several people have spoken to me about the helplessness they feel living or working with someone who is chronically down. One woman described a close colleague as "low-grade depressed, like a battery that's not quite dead but not turning over either."

What makes the situation worse, in her view, is that he seems incapable of taking action, either because he has become so used to how he is, or because whatever he's tried in the past had little effect. Pessimism is symptomatic of a low mood; it can also entrench it.

Another person, an older man, talked to me about how painful it is for him to witness the irritation his own son constantly exhibits and how badly the whole family suffers from the younger man's moods, complaints, agitation and outbursts.

· · ·

WHEN IT IS our own mood that is adversely affecting the people around us, we can take action. And everyone will benefit. When it's a beloved partner, parent or child who is stuck, our choices may feel far more limited and our feelings of helplessness can be hard to bear.

We will feel anxious, perhaps, or impatient and frustrated. And perhaps we face some kind of taboo on tough and truthful talking. We don't want to add to the sufferer's pain by speaking frankly. Nor do we want to provoke an outburst. Ignoring our own pain, it becomes easy to lose touch with a more positive reality.

COMING TO GRIPS with the idea that moods are affected by biology *and* habits of thinking might shift our ideas about change. In his book *Listening to Prozac*, psychiatrist Peter D. Kramer commented on how some people with chronically low or flat moods came to feel their most fundamental sense of self had been restored when medication and therapy worked effectively. What struck Kramer was that while his patients had in most cases not previously known a lively and optimistic adult self, *something within them eagerly claimed it.*

Prozac, or any other medication, is not for everyone. And Kramer does not suggest that. But the evidence has long been in that, intelligently used, therapy and/or medication can make a powerful difference. They can save lives as well as change them.

What can also make a difference—especially when the situation is less drastic—is to challenge the habits of response that most obviously defeat us. Rather than focusing on the monster mood itself (or obsessing fruitlessly on how we got to be this way), *we can choose to act positively, almost regardless of how we feel.*

Let me explain what I mean. Feeling low can and usually does make us unusually self-involved and inwardly lethargic, even while we may also feel agitated or irritable. Noticing that is a vital first step. Taking responsibility for behaving differently, and with greater thoughtfulness and consideration *for others*, is even more transformative.

As we act differently, our feelings will change. Often this means engaging far more energetically than usual with other people, ideas, events, nature and the myriad physical aspects of life that can both stimulate and heal us. And persisting even when it's the last thing we feel like. It also means noticing more keenly what other people need and want, rather than dwelling too closely on our own state of mind. It means responding to what's happening and what's needed on the "outside," rather than being dictated to by our sometimes despotic emotions.

FOR THE SUPPORTERS of someone suffering from chronic low moods, it may mean "rescuing" less often, without in any way being unkind. It may mean caring more but feeling less overwhelmed or defeated. While the moody person may do best by responding *more* consciously to other people's reality, your task may be almost the opposite: asserting your needs more confidently, rather than feeling that they and you must always come second.

It is precisely when throwing ourselves more completely into life seems counterintuitive or plain impossible that it is most urgently needed: restoring and renewing sufferers and supporters alike.

Fit for Life?

How emotionally fit do you feel? Are you ready for whatever life brings, both what is welcome and what is less so? Do you regard yourself confidently? Or are you burdened with misgivings?

Emotional fitness (resourcefulness, robustness, resilience) is something we talk about far less often and with much less assurance than physical fitness. Perhaps this is because the measures of physical fitness are more familiar as well as more obvious. Yet the measures and ideals of emotional fitness are pretty noticeable to us also, or should be.

None of us comes into life fully fit emotionally. Life itself will be our best teacher and coach, if we allow that. The lessons we will learn will depend not only on our experiences but also and most particularly on *what we make of them*. A capacity and willingness to reflect and learn from whatever happens to us is characteristic of the emotionally fit.

It's evident that we don't all start from the same place. We may be lucky enough to have inherited a relatively serene temperament. We may be an optimist by nature or blessed with gifts of insight and empathy. We may have grown up in a family and culture that explicitly invites us to consider other people's well-being and to take responsibility for our own behavior.

As life continues, we may find we're easily capable of enjoying our work and relationships, of giving time to what's pleasurable and inwardly rewarding and of sharing our enthusiasms liberally. We might also be able to soothe ourselves effectively when we are afraid, or are facing a situation that daunts us. All of that contributes to mental and emotional well-being. So does getting through tough situations. Riding the storms, we become a little more storm-proof.

Yet emotional fitness also depends on what we *do* with whatever gifts we have. And how thoughtfully we make them our own. What we do with our gifts will also include how we compensate for what may have been lacking earlier in our lives. This is where mental fortitude plays its part: *noticing what qualities you want to develop* and making them part of your daily behaviors.

Emotional fitness also includes and depends upon the qualities of self-confidence, hope and purpose. How resilient you are radically affects how you will interpret life to yourself on a minute-by-minute basis. Your attitudes arise from and reflect those interpretations.

SOMETIMES IT'S EASIER to get a fix on what our optimum levels of emotional fitness could be by considering what a lack of such fitness looks like. The list of what *undermines* emotional fitness is long but often what dominates is chronic fear or pessimism, a sense you've been particularly hard done by or that others have luck but you do not.

Self-absorption, a lack of genuine interest in other people and an unwillingness or incapacity to see anyone else's point of view are also part of the not-so-fit picture. It will undoubtedly include bad temper and frustration and the delusion that you are entitled to dump those bad moods on others. It will certainly take in the "everyday" addictions of alcohol, recreational drugs, cigarettes, junk food and gambling, or mindless sex. It can emerge in extreme competitiveness, or in a lack of ability to commit to anything or anyone, or to do what needs to be done whether or not you feel like it.

Feeling entitled to blame or dump on others contrasts sharply with the self-responsibility and sense of inner empowerment and choice that come when you feel at least relatively self-accepting (and your behavior reflects that).

Many of us quite unthinkingly talk to or about ourselves in breathtakingly negative and disheartening ways. This seriously undermines our emotional health and often our physical health also.

What's more, negative interpretations will always spill over into how we think about *other* people and their feelings and behaviors. We risk attributing less than ideal motivations to them ("He wants me to fail. . . . "), and we will often feel as though everything we do has the potential to be wrong, or to shame us, or to make us look stupid. This will seriously undermine the pleasure and confidence we have in ourselves and in our own imperfect, precious existence.

To BRING OURSELVES into a more realistic, encouraging relationship with others, we must find ways to feel trustworthy and authentic *from the inside out*. This means taking emotional fitness seriously, and the quality of life it allows. We need to trust where our thinking takes us, and feel in charge of our moods, rather than ruled by them. It will be our choice whether we do this through sharpening our own insights and reflections or by seeking and accepting help.

EMOTIONAL FITNESS lets us feel more alert and confident and more fully alive. It lets us trust our instincts and make decisions without too much anguish. It helps us get over our disappointment when things go wrong. It also lets us see the truths of our shared existence. And it lets us understand the limitations of our precious independence. Yes, we are responsible for who we are becoming and for all that we do, but we also all need and depend upon the kindness and consideration of other people. We can afford to be grateful for that.

As we grow up and look around us, it becomes ever easier to join the kindness dance, to give gracefully and easily and to receive and affirm the kindness of others—even when they haven't quite read our minds or followed our preferred agenda.

Always Powerful

W hether our moods are buoyant or despairing, high, low or somewhere in between, we rarely keep them to ourselves. No matter how powerless we may feel, the power we wield through our moods is tremendous.

Our moods create the atmosphere that we inevitably exude. And, if you doubt me, think about how instantly you can sense if someone is in a bad mood. Or in a terrific one. To go into a room where someone is seething or sulking, no words need be spoken before you want to ask, "What's wrong?" Wordless moods can be used to control other people, terrify or intimidate them. But, equally, our great moods can also be contagious, lifting others' spirits, making them feel alive and appreciated.

Children, animals and most adults are highly sensitive to other people's moods. How odd, then, that so many of us persist with the delusion that our moods (like our thoughts) are our secret: that they are locked up inside our head! That's never true. All but the most psychologically dense (or self-absorbed) will read our moods instantly. They may not always be correct. Perhaps our sadness is mistaken for sullenness; perhaps our exasperation with our partner is mistaken for hostility; perhaps our gaiety is covering our insecurity.

Nonetheless, reading moods—and checking them out—is a vital aspect of our self-understanding as well as of our mutual understanding and care.

OUR MOODS are largely dictated by our thoughts and interpretations as well as the swirl of feelings that accompany them. We may believe our moods are dependent on "things going well," but while events outside ourselves and other people's behavior will always affect us, what's even more crucial is how we *interpret* those events and their impact on us, and the inner commentary we spin around this.

Each of us, without exception, is constantly talking ourselves up or down. We are seeing life and interpreting events through an internal prism that we can easily mistake as factual. When we are in a bad mood, our thinking will reflect that—and reinforce it. As I carefully describe in my book, *Choosing Happiness*, at worst, "bad mood thinking" will make us paranoid, suspicious, aggressive and accusatory. It may also make us self-pitying. It will, at the very least, keep us focused on what's wrong. It will make us unappreciative. It will make us hard to be around.

CHRONIC BAD MOODS—and bad mood thinking—demand and need professional help. They may be a symptom of a mood disorder, depression or persistent anxiety. These are all states of mind where psychotherapy and medication can make a significant difference. This will improve if not transform all aspects of your life, not just mood but also concentration, your capacity to relax and sleep, your physical health, your interactions with other people and how positively and hopefully you think about life itself.

Recognizing that moods don't arrive from outer space but arise within us, we can begin to see ourselves as something other than their victim. This will also help us to monitor the effect of our moods on other people, further inspiring positive action. Most crucial of all, we will understand that we can and must take responsibility for the thoughts and interpretations that drive our moods.

Whatever our fluctuations in mood, we take a vital first step when we begin to ask: "What stories am I constantly telling myself? How are they lifting my mood or lowering it? Does the way I routinely interpret events or other people's behavior help them—or me? Do I know what will move a 'bad mood' into a better one?"

CHOOSING TO BECOME increasingly aware of how we are affecting other people through our moods—and all that moods express—takes real strength of character as well as of mind. It may even take courage. But to experience that we do not need to be the victim of our own negative moods, or slaves to our unhelpful attitudes or habits of thinking, is utterly liberating.

Hungry Minds

Over the past couple of decades, and with increasing speed, our understanding of that most vital organ—the brain—has changed dramatically. The pioneering science of neuroplasticity is showing for the first time that the brain is able to regenerate itself in ways that few could have imagined and most of us can still barely comprehend.

We have long known what a magnificent and complex organ the brain is. What we didn't know was how "plastic" it also is and how capable it is of significantly reorganizing itself when "it" or its environment needs that.

. In fact, far from being fixed in its capacities, by the time you reach your late twenties, the brain can retrieve losses, build new strengths and, in quite awesome ways, repair itself. With stimulation, it will literally grow weightier.

This is great news for people whose brains have been damaged through illness or accidents and for those struggling with learning and motor skill difficulties or cognitive deficits. It may in time also be good news for people who suffer from psychiatric illnesses. And it is certainly good news for anyone who fears that getting older inevitably means losing "brain power" or closing down. Brain anatomy *and* behavior are open to positive change: that's a powerful message.

In his widely praised book, *The Brain That Changes Itself,* Canadian psychoanalyst and neuroscientist Norman Doidge calls these fresh insights "one of the most extraordinary discoveries of the twentieth century." Doidge may be wrong. It may turn out to be one of the most extraordinary discoveries of *any* century. But meanwhile our knowledge of the mind is still lagging.

Mind and brain are inextricably linked. Healthy minds depend on more than the brain but certainly can't function well when the brain is not in good shape. What's utterly fascinating is that the converse is also true.

Let me explain what I mean. For its optimum health, our brain depends on our mind being used in active and dynamic ways, ideally taking us repeatedly "outside the box" of constrained or habitual responses and thinking.

In *The Brain That Changes Itself,* Doidge explains how the brain functions like a series of maps. This makes more sense if you remember that it's so much more difficult to learn a second or third language in adulthood than when you "picked it up" as a child. That remains true, but not because the brain has become too rigid, as was previously thought, but rather because the "map" for language learning has come to be dominated by the person's increasing control of their primary language.

By contrast, when a child learns two or more languages simultaneously that particular map within the brain shares those languages and the library of sounds and meaning that deliver language. This affirms the value of early learning but again doesn't lead to a fixed scenario. Artificial stimulation of the part of the brain known as the nucleus basalis may eventually lead to adults learning languages and other information as effortlessly as children do, or relearning how to read and write after accidents or illness. In the meantime, learning something stimulating and difficult—at whatever age—does much more than give you extra skills. It also improves your thinking and brain health more generally, driving healthy "plastic change."

As SOMEONE who reads, writes and researches for her living as well as pleasure, this optimistic view thrills me. And for all of us, scholars or not, it creates an irresistible imperative: use the mind to grow the brain, taking it not to the old limits only but to the alluring frontiers of the new. In fact, when we don't stretch, test and exercise the mind, when we don't *use* the complex and myriad faculties of the mind, *the brain suffers*. The person suffers. Society suffers. Capacities within the brain that are damaged or even destroyed can be regenerated. We know that. But capacities within the brain that are creaky from disuse will simply degenerate. We also know that.

INVESTING IN our minds on a lifelong basis is the greatest service we can do for our brains and continuing overall quality of life. Investing in our minds *and* brains is better than a good idea: it makes absolute sense. This more than justifies giving up whatever clouds or obliterates our thinking, including recreational drugs, junk food or daily alcohol consumption. It also means getting some detachment and insight about *how* we think as well as what we think about.

As any child could tell us, *boredom is bad for the brain*. Bored or shut down for long enough and we will drift dangerously close to depression. But constant agitation is also harmful and will be no substitute for the real excitement that comes with pursuing something with interest and curiosity.

The human mind is hungry for genuinely stimulating experiences and, conversely, for genuine rest when it's tired. Junk food for the mind is at least as harmful as junk food for the body. Junk for the mind might include constant noise and eruptions, the pseudostimulation of hours of television or computer games, and the stressful agitation of gambling machines.

One of the changes I have noticed with getting older is that I am also increasingly intolerant of the empty noise of loud music in every shopping mall that I visit.

Noise can be extremely harmful to the mind, both the noise and the effort it takes to tune it out.

WHEN IT COMES to using and developing the mind's capacities, a supportive social environment makes all the difference. A child's natural curiosity is one of their greatest gifts. It deserves to be nourished. So does their appetite for awe as well as learning. How that capacity is nurtured, and how much experience is firsthand, rather than seen through a screen or on a page, will make a profound difference in each individual child's life. This doesn't depend on money or privilege. Nor is it about cleverness or the capacity to reproduce other people's ideas or mimic their opinions.

In Antibes in the South of France, the ideal place for such a purchase, I bought a black canvas bag bearing a quote from the painter Henri Matisse: "Il faut regarder toute la vie avec des yeux d'enfant" (It's necessary to look at all of life through the eyes of a child). Today even our youngest children are sometimes discouraged in their natural creativity, originality and curiosity. But when we shut those aptitudes down in a child we limit their minds as well as their brains. We make their lives smaller and much less joyful. We make our lives smaller also.

WHATEVER OUR AGE or circumstances the ideal environment for the mind and brain allows for freshness, originality, curiosity, creativity, sensual as well as intellectual explorations, risk, and a willing and constant testing of new ideas. When those qualities and activities are not available, the mind slackens and life feels sour.

Even the most thoughtful people need to shake up their preconceptions on a regular basis. Examining what you have "always thought," listening to a range of opinions, taking the plunge to learn and experience something new and (ideally) tough and challenging, will get your thoughts whirling. It will also get your spirits rising. Your mind and your brain will benefit. So will your life.

The Moody Brain

Do you know what might motivate you to make significant changes in what and how you eat, particularly if you had to give up some familiar short-term pleasures?

Vanity, or a fear of being fat or fatter, often gives people a needed push. I know that's been a powerful motivator for me. But making changes on that basis can easily feel like deprivation. And that, in turn, makes change much harder to sustain. Those prompts don't help thin people, either, who may be eating just as badly. So size is not the only issue here.

In fact, what may encourage you to eat more thoughtfully, and with much more pleasure, is simply noticing which foods lift your mood and energy levels and which foods lower them. This is particularly significant if you think how tempting it often is to eat the worst foods (fatty, sweet, empty of nutrients) when you are already feeling low.

SOME PSYCHOLOGICALLY minded naturopaths and doctors and a few gastroenterologists have been talking for years now about the links between nutrition and emotional well-being, but it's a much less popular conversation in psychological and psychiatric circles. Neuroscientist and psychiatrist Daniel G. Amen, M.D., discusses food among many other issues in his book *Change Your Brain, Change Your Life*. But he's a rarity.

This makes academic studies on the topic of nutrition and mental health even more exciting. I came across two that each point to significant increases in emotional well-being when patients with quite severe mental health issues were treated with dietary supplements.

The first study was carried out at Canterbury University in New Zealand. It involved adult patients who had both attention deficit/hyperactivity disorder (ADHD) and severe mood swings. They were treated with micronutrients, including vitamins, minerals and amino acids. At the end of an eight-week period their depression had fallen into the "normal nondepressed range." They also showed significant improvements on measures of hyperactivity, anxiety, impulsivity and overall quality of life.

If you have suffered from depression or ADHD yourself, or have witnessed someone else struggling with these illnesses, you will know that any improvement is cause for celebration. This is particularly true when it's achieved without side effects. Two months later, those in the sample who had continued with the nutrients had further improved while those who did not continue were again experiencing adverse symptoms.

It was a small trial and will be easily dismissed by skeptics. But less than a couple of weeks later I read of an Australian trial at the University of Melbourne's Orygen research center where fish oil supplements were used to treat young people identified as being in danger of developing psychosis or schizophrenia.

Forty-one patients at risk were given four fish oil capsules a day for three months. Only two went on to develop a psychotic disorder, in contrast with eleven out of forty in the control group. What's more, because there were again no side effects, patients stayed with the program. This is particularly encouraging for young people because antipsychotic drugs can have awful side effects including weight gain and sexual dysfunction, adding another blow to fragile self-confidence and self-esteem.

IT WOULD BE FOOLISH to suggest that improved nutrition will be the sole or primary answer to everyday misery or for more serious mental illnesses. I'm also well aware how hard it is to persuade someone else to eat better in order to feel better. Yet whether we are struggling or well, it seems shameful to ignore how directly food affects mood.

I'm entirely persuaded that what we drink as well as what we eat makes a massive difference to energy levels, levels of calm or irritability and overall well-being, and to mood. But your most convincing answers will come from the nearest and most accurate laboratory of all: your own body and life.

Good Mood Food

How you think, the attitudes you choose to develop, your values, interpretations and perspective on life are what will affect your mood and outlook most. There's great comfort in that because those are all aspects of living we can control.

There's another area of our lives where we can also take charge of our moods and emotional vibrancy, and that's with the foods we eat. If your brain is short of vital nutrients or water it cannot function optimally, and neither can you.

Food, or nutritional supplements, will never be the complete answer when it comes to issues of emotional or physical well-being. Quite obviously you are affected by genes and by events outside yourself (and how you interpret them) as well as by what you eat. Nevertheless, it is unquestionably worth noticing what's going into your mouth, recognizing that it has immediate effects on the brain (and therefore on well-being) and monitoring whether it is undermining or supporting you.

Attention to the brain is the place to start. Water makes up 85 percent of your brain's weight. Keeping it adequately hydrated is a vital first step. Water throughout the day makes a difference not just to mood but also to memory, energy and concentration.

Your brain needs 25 percent of your body's oxygen so protein-rich foods are also vital for oxygen-carrying iron and for providing the essential amino acid tryptophan, which supports healthy brain function. Tryptophan is a precursor in the central nervous system of the neurotransmitter serotonin, which affects both mood and sleep. Most antidepressant medications boost serotonin, but gaining tryptophan from food eliminates the side effects that sometimes come with medication.

You can easily research for yourself which foods are helpful in this area, but soy products are a great start not only because there are now so many of them but also because soy additionally provides choline, another neurotransmitter nutrient.

Cottage cheese, chicken and turkey breast, nuts, seeds and bananas are easily included in the optimum mental health diet. And it's worth knowing that the glucose supplied by complex carbohydrates literally fuels the brain. This means a breakfast of oatmeal, rice or whole-grain bread along with fruit or juice will give you a welcome serotonin boost a few hours later, just when people who have skipped breakfast or eaten sugary foods are already flagging.

Dark leafy greens, broccoli and asparagus, blueberries and strawberries are also stars in the good mood diet. So are the omega-3 fatty acids. Main sources are cold-water fish like salmon, mackerel, herring or tuna, with reports suggesting that the more fish a country eats, the lower its rates of depression. (The studies I refer to in the previous chapter give additional weight to this proposition.)

Flaxseed oil is an alternative source for vegetarians but, as with all things, moderation is essential and consulting a psychologically minded nutritionist or naturopath before making significant changes is essential.

THERE IS increasing interest also in the proposition that folic acid (folate) and B vitamins impact mood. Just as interesting is the suggestion that a deficiency of B vitamins can produce a toxic protein called homocysteine that may possibly increase your chances of developing depression or Alzheimer's. The jury is out on that, but meanwhile leafy green vegetables, asparagus and broccoli plus whole grains, nuts, seeds, and pulses and soy products, again, are broadly beneficial, along with lean red meat, prawns, chicken, raisins and apricots.

A deficiency of selenium has also been linked to depression. Brazil nuts provide an easy remedy and, again, only modest quantities are needed to be helpful.

EATING FRESH, varied foods and drinking lots of water seems a literally delicious way to support your brain and all its complex functions, while also supporting your mood and emotions. Those are the same foods that will also benefit your skin, your weight, your energy levels—in fact, your entire well-being. But if those foods have to compete with lots of junk—fatty, highly processed, "empty" or sugar-laden foods—your best efforts will be undone.

It's essential to understand that junk, as well as caffeine and alcohol, keeps you vulnerable to mood swings, exhaustion, irritability and cravings, however healthily you otherwise eat. Caffeine needs to be reduced gradually to avoid side effects. But sugar cravings can be quickly eased with yet more whole grains, green beans, nuts, peanut butter, prunes, seafood and potatoes, all of which contain chromium, a magical ingredient that reduces sugar cravings. Chromium can be bought as a supplement. However, the foods in which it naturally occurs bring many other benefits, the whole picture giving "eating for pleasure" a particularly tasty spin.

Too Tired to Care

❅

If you are too exhausted to be pleasant, or so exhausted that any additional demand makes you want to lie down and weep, then this is not a problem with moods. It's far more fundamental than that. It gets down to what you think your life is for, how you are "spending" it, who you think you need to please, and how you are conserving and expending your energy.

In the busiest of lives—and there are few lives busier than if you are the parent of young children or if you are a carer—there are still and always choices to be made.

SOMETIMES IT HELPS to identify and even write down which tasks particularly exhaust you and resolve to do the bare minimum of those, or to get help so that they feel less onerous. You may be responding to standards that are unrealistic. You might be addicted to being in control and doing things your way. You might feel you have no right to ask for help or that you will only be disappointed by the kind of help you would be given.

Writing down your needs or wishes, and also writing down your thoughts or inner commentary about those needs, can be surprisingly clarifying (I describe this process in much more detail in my book *Creative Journal Writing*). It lets you see your situation more clearly. And that alone immediately gives you a renewed sense of choice. It also saves you from feeling helpless as well as overwhelmed.

This doesn't mean that all your needs will be met. Sometimes it's enough to acknowledge them and to recognize that some of those desires or wishes ("If only the baby would sleep through the night") belong within a time frame that is always changing. What is often crucial is just recognizing that you can, indeed, let some things go. You can do less and care more. You can allow other people to do some things for or with you, rather than doing "everything" yourself. You can answer back when your mind says, "It's hopeless."

Learning to receive help from others is essential to living kindly and well. Independence is a great thing but we are all, every one of us, also dependent on others, both directly and indirectly. Becoming *someone who is easy to help* and *even easier to please* is itself an achievement. It also makes it far less difficult or complicated to give to others without feeling begrudging or depleted.

While you are looking with a clear eye at your life, you might also want to ask who you think you are pleasing, running so fast that it makes you tired. You might need to ask whether being constantly busy and exhausted is saving you from something (boredom, a feeling of being useless), or even justifying your entire existence. These are hard questions to ask and answer but the price of avoiding them is very high.

THE OLD ADAGE about the mythical Jack—*All work and no play makes Jack a dull boy*—comes in here. When conducting your mini-audit on what has been wearing you down, it is just as essential to be at least as clear about what sustains or uplifts you, and to see honestly how much time you are devoting to those precious moments.

We will sail through the exhausting but necessary tasks with far greater ease when our life doesn't feel like a ceaseless round of chores. There has to be time for what delights us, lifts our spirits, makes us laugh, allows us to be silly and unself-conscious. There has to be time and eagerness for what makes work, and especially parenting or caring for others, a joy as well as a responsibility. There has to be time for relishing our physical existence, the world around us and the social worlds of family, community and friends. There has to be time for grace, beauty, awe: gifts of the spirit.

GIVING YOURSELF permission to enjoy and appreciate your life more will be such a relief to everyone who knows you, and especially those who most love you. You might even make some changes first for their sake. But you, too, will richly benefit.

Pleasure and Play

❁

When we are thoroughly delighted, enthused or excited we hardly need to inquire about the state of our minds or moods. Yet delight, pleasure and play all take a lesser place in our earnest and work-focused lives than perhaps they should.

Work is not the only impediment to pleasure. (Work may even be a genuine source of companionship and stimulation and the pleasure they bring.) Leisure can also cause us problems, or create a problem we don't know how to solve.

One of the most interesting discoveries I made when researching *Choosing Happiness* is just how closely "not-happiness" (feeling depressed, anxious, disengaged, hostile, helpless) can be linked to being understimulated or just plain bored. While we may be making time for ourselves, our ideas about relaxing and refreshing ourselves could be wildly off the mark.

Sit in front of mindless television shows for long and you are likely to get up feeling empty or exhausted. Fill your holidays with nothing but sand and trashy novels and you may come home feeling irritable. Have the same predictable conversations repeatedly with your loved ones and you are likely to be bored as well as boring.

Rerun the same limited ideas in the privacy of your own mind and the world will also seem grim.

This is great news because once we accept that our wondrous minds actually need to be nourished, stretched, challenged, intrigued and enchanted—as well as sometimes genuinely rested—*we can do something about it.*

Pleasure in the natural world, time for play, enthusiasms and all kinds of physical activity wholly support well-being. But that's not enough. Staying open to new intellectual and mental challenges throughout your life, creating opportunities for stimulating discoveries at work and away from it, facing change with interest, cultivating the ability to think freshly and independently, and risking having your opinions changed, are all mind-care basics.

Reading something that is stretching or intellectually provocative; becoming a beginner again with something that is challenging to learn; finding companions in your interests: these are initiatives within reach of most people (and need not be at all costly). They are a priceless investment not only in a lively future, but also in a lively present moment.

So is experiencing the world through your senses: tasting the food you are eating; rejoicing in the dazzling variety of colors the world offers; letting yourself notice the feel of morning sun or afternoon rain on your skin; relishing the touch of a friend's hand or the softness of a baby's cheek; taking time to listen to music, not as background only but with your complete attention; throwing off inhibitions to dance, sing, speak poetry out loud; making time for new or old rituals, for silence, for deep and sacred listening; time to remember what life is *for.*

. . .

THE BEST COMPANIONS in the world are open to new experiences, new ideas, and to beauty. They are widely interested as well as interesting, sharp and well filled yet with room to grow. And even while they are looking forward, they are unafraid to rejoice in the moment.

Such people are not ageless; they improve with age. It's a fate we can share.

Last Call

❋

One of the markers of Western society—and one that appalls many people from more traditional cultures—is that it is considered acceptable and sometimes even admirable to drink alcohol to excess.

People who choose to limit their drinking are often mocked or pilloried. As I was writing this I read in the newspaper an account of a well-known Sydney art dealer who refuses to invite people to his famous lunches who don't drink alcohol or don't drink it on every possible occasion. When Midnight Oil musician-turned-politician Peter Garrett went to one of these lunches and drank only water he apparently lost his chance of being invited back.

I loathe such attitudes and the ignorance they display. Countless lives are broken, blighted or prematurely ended because of alcohol addiction and abuse. Drinking until you are drunk is still routinely confused with skewed notions of what it means to be a man. And, at every level of society, from the most to the least economically privileged, "celebration" often means some people becoming so drunk they can't remember what they are celebrating. Many parents see excessive drinking as inevitable as their children move into adolescence. Excuses are made for people who are cruel, abusive, violent, irresponsible, sexually promiscuous, uncontrollable and out of control when drunk. And one of the least encouraging changes in recent years is that women's drinking is reaching levels as unhealthy and excessive as those of men.

Yet drinking excessively remains socially acceptable—and lauded. It is even seen to be a rather hilarious aspect of our national psyche and culture, while criticizing excessive drinking and the alcohol culture is seen as prudish, punitive or even unpatriotic.

LIKE EVERY CHILD growing up in the 1950s and 1960s in Australia or New Zealand, I saw the ghastly effects of what used to be called the six o'clock swill. It seems hard to believe now but many men would race to the pub after work, drink in haste in public bars and stagger home drunk. Women who drank, or women and men who drank together, did so in "private bars" where they sat at tables rather than standing in a tiled barn that could be hosed down at a quarter past six.

It was widely assumed in those years that drunkenness was made worse by the limited hours, and that more "civilized" hours would result in more restrained and more pleasurable drinking. That's not the case.

IN TWENTY-FIRST-CENTURY life in Australia alcohol can be bought virtually at any hour and in far more salubrious places, yet this hasn't resulted in fewer people having serious problems with drink, or fewer problems caused by drink. Conservative statistics suggest that in Australia more than 51 percent of alcohol consumed is drunk at levels that pose a risk of short-term (immediate) harm. Sounds reasonable enough?

Well, what about this? More than two million Australians drink at high or risky levels (one in eight adults). More than three thousand Australians die each year as a result of their harmful drinking, almost twice the number of people who die on the roads. When factors such as crime and violence are taken into account, as well as treatment costs, loss of productivity and premature death, alcohol abuse is costing our community more than fifteen billion dollars annually.

And how should we measure the social costs? It is not easy, although a study published in the *American Journal of Public Health* reported that in the United States up to 28 percent of children are exposed to alcohol dependence or abuse in a family situation at some time before the age of eighteen.

As WITH ANY ADDICTION, the reasons why people drink excessively are complex. Alcohol is a depressant. That's widely known. It affects every vital organ in the body, including the brain. Yet for many people drinking is a way to deal with their least welcome, least comfortable feelings. Alcohol tastes good. It appears to be an effective buffer against anxiety, depression, confusion, isolation and self-doubt.

It's still far more acceptable to get drunk when you have problems than to make an effort to understand your problems and do something about them. Looking into a glass for salvation is apparently easier than facing yourself. It's also far less likely to be publicly derided.

For many chronic drinkers, the next drink is the only one that counts. Even the medium-term effects of drinking are lost on people when the need for a drink seems compelling. Alcohol lets people feel less inhibited, less self-conscious and often far more sociable. Many people literally can't imagine enduring a social occasion without a drink in their hand. Quite quickly alcohol also makes people irritable, sloppy, unreliable and sometimes dangerously aggressive. But as their faculties of judgment subside, the way they judge themselves also changes.

I AM INCREASINGLY convinced that people drink far too much in most Western countries not because we are leading carefree, fun-filled lives but because we are seriously short of inner spirit and real pleasure. We are also a highly self-conscious lot, vulnerable to other people's opinions and may be far less inwardly robust than many of us would like to believe.

Drinking to excess, people may get a welcome rest from their own self-doubt and inner critic. Those rewards, as well as the powerful social rituals that surround drinking, are hard to give up. That means that in a country where alcohol flows virtually wherever people gather, the courage to stand apart from the drinking frenzy is seldom supported.

It's easy to understand why. People who drink excessively often react strongly to what they interpret as other people's actual or potential judgments. If you are the person who is refusing a drink or doesn't want to drink (as I know personally), a committed drinker is quite likely to take that refusal as an implicit rebuke of their choices and react defensively. This is not neutral territory. Feelings for and against alcohol run high. Because there is so much pressure to drink—and not to be seen as a teetotaler or wet blanket—it takes real strength to step away from the drinking culture, particularly if it was once a constant in your life or was your favored way of dealing with social occasions.

WE KNOW NOW that alcohol is disastrous for young people when it's consumed in even quite mild amounts. It also has deleterious effects on people who have been diagnosed with a range of illnesses, including cancer. (So perhaps it's safe to assume that beyond a glass or two per week, it has deleterious effects. Period.)

When I talk about alcohol consumption to people who have had breast cancer, through my work with Breast Cancer Network Australia, I often suggest that when drinking less or no alcohol feels difficult for someone it can be very helpful to reflect on what alcohol is giving them. Is it taste? If that's the case, could they get delicious, pleasurable taste sensations in other, more nourishing ways? Is it stress relief? Or boldness and ease in social situations?

Again, there are many ways far more effective to reduce stress and increase confidence than having another drink. To discover that you are not dependent on drinking alcohol is liberating. Discovering that, it becomes far easier to put up with other people's awkwardness and disparaging remarks.

WHEN SOMEONE'S drinking is more than "social," Alcoholics Anonymous continues to be a brilliant haven. Other people affirm the daily effort it takes not to drink. Living a sober life becomes a new reality.

It's also possible for each in our own modest way to influence the culture in which alcohol is consumed. Families with children and adolescents need to show by example how easy it is to have a good time without constant drinking. They could model alcohol-free days. They could also make it clear that emotional problems are worsened and not solved by alcohol. And that far from being a sign of maturity, excessive drinking is like a billboard declaring that ordinary life is more than you can cope with.

DRINKERS WHO are determined to go on "drowning their sorrows" could at the very least back off from criticizing those who don't drink or who drink modestly. They could also support those attempting to drink less by acknowledging that this is a worthwhile choice and curbing their urges to deride and mock.

Men as well as women could choose to develop far healthier ways to name and deal with their emotional challenges. At social occasions we could make sure we have something more interesting to offer nondrinkers than mineral water and orange juice. We could take seriously the effects of alcohol on brains, bodies, social lives and relationships. We could take the loss of life seriously, the loss of dignity, the families and communities damaged by alcohol or even destroyed. We could refuse to romanticize excessive drinking, or make heroes out of drunks. We could talk about drinking differently and more truthfully so that social and cultural pressures would lean toward moderate rather than excessive drinking. We could stop normalizing rites of passage that are alcohol fueled. We could look hard at what more meaningfully sustains our lives and relationships—and revalue that.

· · ·

THESE ARE CHANGES that are difficult for individuals to make. They are especially difficult for people who are already struggling with issues of social acceptance and self-confidence. They would be far more possible and powerful, as well as more effective, if they were made collectively. But do we have the mettle, the heart or the will to make them? I'm doubtful.

Tipping Points

❈

I think it's fair to say that virtually everyone has a tipping point when it comes to losing their cool or "blowing their top." Even the Dalai Lama, apparently, can be sharp when needed. The trouble with the chronically bad tempered though is that even a trivial setback will set them off. And sometimes there is no setback at all. Some of this will be caused by general stress and made worse by anxiety that's not addressed. Exhaustion or hunger adds to the brew. So does entrenched pessimistic or catastrophic thinking.

There's no doubt either that alcohol markedly affects people's self-control. What's more, it irritates the central nervous system, and irritation, like frustration, is key to the bad-temper picture. Grumpy, angry, morbid, reactive and tense people would all do better avoiding alcohol completely.

THERE IS ANOTHER FACTOR, too, that's best summed up as a sense of entitlement. In some families and cultures it is simply not permissible to explode at the least or even the greatest provocation. But someone who is routinely exploding will almost always have an internal sense of permission—even if it's unconscious.

Popular psychology has some responsibility here. For several decades many therapists and psychologists argued that outbursts were "healthier" than repression and that if people were free to express their emotions, including hostility or anger, they were less likely to be depressed.

That theory is, thankfully, now largely discounted. It is far more useful to see that rage or irritability may be symptoms of depression. In adolescents especially, such symptoms should be taken seriously. But relief for depression or any mood disorder won't come through expressing negative or hostile feelings ever more freely. In fact, the opposite is true.

Bad temper expresses a frustration that something is out of our control or isn't the way we want it to be. The irony is, of course, that in the explosive person this failure of external control stimulates a lack of internal control, worsening a sense of inner helplessness or chaos. And what makes it worse is that when you feel entitled to explode and have no internal censor, you will certainly find more and more to explode about.

TAKING CHARGE of the harm caused by chronic bad temper is the place to start. Few people want to spread their unhappiness or cause others to feel frightened in their presence. Those are destructive choices *but must be seen as choices if any degree of change is to be achieved*.

Even the most reactive people will control themselves in some situations. Observing what those situations are can bring a new sense of control more broadly. What makes it possible to be calmer at the office, for example? Or when you are with friends? What makes it easier to problem-solve more effectively? When are you

looking for solutions most actively? How would you soothe someone else in a tight spot? What could replace alcohol as a way to
relax? Or junk food as a source of comfort?

These patterns and choices quickly build a most useful picture.
As patterns of ease and reaction become clearer, and as triggers can
be more easily anticipated and avoided, the most habitually reactive
person will be well on the way to gaining the self-respect and ease
that come with exercising choice. They will also be relishing the
benefits.

WORK

✺

Work and Love

※

It's easy to overvalue the work we do. Or perhaps just the time it takes. It is just as easy to demean or undervalue other people's efforts and contributions.

Two classic examples stand out. The first is when people equate what they are paid with the value of their work. The second is when someone's work is unpaid—and its value is ignored or questioned.

IN THE FIRST INSTANCE, most of us know that earning lots of money solves some problems very nicely, but may create others. In my experience, "doing exceptionally well" does not automatically accelerate self-inquiry and self-awareness or even generosity, at least not until those people are pushed by life to discover for themselves that wealth, prestige and others' envy truly does not answer all their prayers.

The second and far more common situation is when someone's work is largely unpaid, unceasing—and undervalued or not valued at all.

A day caring for others doesn't fill a time sheet neatly. More often than not, much of the care is as invisible as it is necessary.

Even when the day has been ceaselessly demanding, it is difficult to find a cheery, convincing answer to the ghastly question, "What did you do all day?"

This work—which is far more likely to be done by women than men—rarely comes to an end when night falls. It requires a depth of patience and fortitude that few paid jobs could match. Yet it is notable for its lack of applause, "time out," bonuses, promotion and the company of colleagues. It is also notable for the kindness that it demands and the appreciation it often lacks.

Some men (and by no means all) can be totally crass in overlooking or trivializing what is being done at home, a place they may think of primarily as somewhere to relax, rather than as somewhere to share the responsibilities and chores as well as the joys. The complexity of emotional work is easily ignored. So is the constancy of housework and childcare. So is the ceaseless juggle of combining paid and unpaid work in what can seem like unmanageable amounts.

Women, too, can hurt and punish with their disinterest. They can be envious or resentful about what they perceive as their partner's or friends' easier access to paid work. They can be so consumed by their own resentments that it becomes difficult to validate their partner's efforts. They can also be angry and belittling because their partner is not as successful as they would like him to be.

How PEOPLE WORK, and particularly how they think about work—paid and unpaid—will inevitably impact on every intimate relationship. When this is not understood, and when each person is not validated, affirmed and appreciated for their efforts, the relationship will suffer. *Everyone* will suffer.

. . .

MEN AND WOMEN share a conscious and unconscious vulnerability about work, even when this is understood and expressed in different ways. When someone's paid work is insecure, tough or unrewarding, work will feel like a burden whatever its volume, its rewards or its prestige. Highly competitive workplaces can be hell for many people; so can work that is dirty, dull or dangerous; or work that involves any form of service to an often brutally rude public.

Even when work is easier or more pleasurable, it is at work, and around work, that many of us feel most judged by others. Understanding this vulnerability, and how diversely it may be expressed, means that thinking together about what work asks of us is an honest conversation that couples, friends and families need to have.

WORK IS JUST one part of life. How we think about it, though, how we identify with it, bear its costs, and value each other's efforts as well as the rewards it brings, affects every aspect of our being. Sigmund Freud argued that we need work as much as we need love. We need it for what it can contribute to our lives, socially as well as economically. We need it for the ways it gives structure and meaning to our lives. And we need it for what, through work, we are able to contribute.

Working Wiser

❧

Working in an office was once considered to be clean and relatively healthy. The risks it poses are still a great deal milder than, for example, working in mines or most factories, driving a truck or train, laying carpets, bricklaying, cleaning windows on city skyscrapers or working directly with an unfriendly and often hostile public.

Nonetheless, even the most prestigious and valued work can take a toll on the body. And with the levels of stress and exhaustion that are commonplace, it can easily take a toll also on the emotions and spirit. As we age, work may become more rather than less difficult. And that makes it essential that if we want to extend our years of work and enjoy it, we consider seriously what meaning work has for us and what will allow us to work with increasing rather than decreasing rewards.

SOME YEARS AGO in the small New South Wales city of Grafton I attended one of the most delightful festivals I have ever experienced. Well-planned, intimate and friendly, it brought together the interdependent disciplines of philosophy, religion and science—already a brilliant concept. But what topped it off was its marvelous location in the beautiful, embracing Grafton Anglican cathedral.

For a few days we writers, philosophers and scientists led an idyllic existence. Thinking *mattered*. Ideas and talking about ideas *mattered*. The presenters talked to each other at length and the lively audiences freely talked to the presenters. The cathedral became the center of everything, much as it might have been in any lively town in medieval times.

One of the writers was the celebrated English priest and theologian John Polkinghorne. And the reason I am telling this story at all is that he was enjoying a second and rather different illustrious career from his first. He had started out as an acclaimed physicist, teaching mathematical physics at Cambridge for years and publishing extensively. Then, in his forties, he moved from professor to student and retrained as a priest.

WHAT'S REMARKABLE HERE is not just that this story nicely challenges the assumption that a brilliant scientist could not also believe in God. Or that it is possible to take a big step down (from professor to student) and still go up! What the story also demonstrates is that while our strengths of mind change as we age, there can be considerable gains as well as losses. And these might allow for new opportunities.

Polkinghorne was clear that in his forties his best work as a physicist was behind him. This was not a reason to move on but presumably it made change less difficult. Mathematics and physics, he claimed, will always be best achieved by the young and brilliant rather than the old and wise. Philosophy and theology (and most serious forms of writing), on the other hand, demand patience, depth of thinking and a broad view, attributes that rarely belong to the young and that can improve with age. Interestingly, this same view of science as a younger person's game is offered in David Leavitt's *The Indian Clerk*, a novel that's far more about mathematics, minds and aging than it is about India or clerks.

MOST OF US WILL never be brilliant or highly praised, no matter how young we now are or how old we may become. Nonetheless wisdom—and the humanity and humility that come with it—remain accessible.

The qualities that John Polkinghorne identified as assets for a world-class theologian can work for anyone at least mildly committed to a life of inquiry. As we age we can, if we choose, grow more and not less curious. We can learn from our mistakes without being crushed by them. We can appreciate what other people have to teach us. We can abandon unhelpful attitudes. We can discover for ourselves that money matters less than happiness and kindness. We can value beauty, passion and good humor. We can open less self-consciously to the spiritual dimension of life and the questions and consolations this brings. And we can certainly develop and cherish the infinite arts of reflection.

IF WE ARE FORTUNATE, we might take this increasing breadth of vision into our workplace, as well as using it in life more generally. This doesn't mean that we will necessarily work harder than we have previously done. Or in a more prestigious career. In fact, it could mean that we choose something far more modest than would once have satisfied us (and our ego). It might also mean that we are prepared, as Dr. Polkinghorne was, to become a beginner again, whatever our age. Or to support, rather than lead. Or to lead from the center rather than the front. Or to value meaning above wealth. Or simply to trust in the wisdom of our own rather than society's urgings.

Smart Work

For many workplace roles, there is surprisingly little training. All kinds of assumptions are routinely made about what people can and will pick up from the work culture and from colleagues. Yet how we interpret what we observe can be highly subjective and may even be wildly inaccurate.

Listening to people over the years, and working with teams in a variety of organizations, I observe that many people work in a kind of fog, afraid to make mistakes, unsure if they are doing things as well as they could, feeling highly sensitive to perceived or actual criticism, yet also critical when other people tackle tasks differently from the way that they would.

We often feel at work as though we are in some kind of competition, not just with our colleagues but also with an imagined idealized worker—and that we are not measuring up.

It's worth standing back from your work on a regular basis to question how you are approaching the details. It's just as valuable to look hard at the bigger picture of your attitudes to work, your need for it and your engagement with it. Those attitudes will make all the difference as to whether your days are pleasant or stimulating, or something to be endured. Resentment of what you are doing, or of what you believe is required of you, will always be debilitating. Uncertainty and a basic lack of confidence are also undermining and will affect the way you relate to other people. You might be overly sensitive to criticism, for example, or regard all instructions and requests as undermining, even when that's not intended. It can be equally unconstructive to be too arrogant about how things should be done. That might blind you to the value of other people's initiatives or creativity; it may block your own creativity.

You might also be limiting yourself with an old story that you are not capable of new challenges. Or that you will always be overlooked. Or that you will be picked for the worst rather than best tasks. What we expect is not inevitably lived out. It does, however, influence our thinking. It may also influence other people's confidence in us.

WHEN WE SHIFT from thinking about the big picture to the smaller details, we may see that much of what we routinely do could be done "smarter," with less anxiety, less fuss or perhaps less unnecessary repetition. Sometimes this means noticing what time is wasted looking for what should be close to hand, or making choices and decisions that could be self-evident, once streamlined. It may also mean noticing that we all have our vulnerable points, as well as strengths. In my own working life, for example, I am fairly comfortable with the intense demands of writing and frequent public speaking but find it hard to keep up with the administration required by my public life. In fact, as I sit here now and think about it, I find the detail needed for my obligatory quarterly financial reporting exceptionally arduous. Really there is not much to it but I am trapped by my own anxiety in a sphere where I feel less than competent. Drilling myself to use quite rigid systems has helped. And I can't believe how long it has taken me to discover the glories of plastic filing sleeves and inviolable filing systems to lessen my fears of losing some vital piece of paper.

Making lists, as well as using Post-it notes (and the calendar on my computer), works for me, too. I have long periods when I don't write lists and simply commit everything that should be on a list to memory. But when I come back to making lists again I feel real satisfaction when at least some of the tasks are completed, as well as being able to see at a glance what is urgent and perhaps what is barely necessary at all.

Checking on what gets in the way of being comfortably decisive is also worth a few minutes' quiet reflection. Making decisions too fast because you can't bear the anxiety of a decision postponed may not be helpful. But procrastination can also be deadly. Again, it helps to question your attitude toward making decisions more generally. And then to inspect with some interest how you are making specific decisions and whether the results are, largely, working for you. You may, for example, make decisions with an eye to pleasing others or causing the least fuss. You may be following a formula or values that are now outdated.

Trusting the decisions we are making can be as arduous as trusting our opinions; we have to learn through persistent practice and reflection. There is no other way.

As WE FEEL more confident about the logistics of work (and let's face it, most people's working lives include countless tasks that are far from exciting), it becomes easier to listen cheerfully to other people's instructions, to notice and learn from the way they do things, and to remain relaxed when someone does something in their way—rather than yours. Perhaps when you are the one who must give an instruction, you will also do it more cheerfully when you feel confident rather than anxious.

This doesn't have to mean letting your standards slip. But it may mean encouraging greater care rather than rebuking. Care for detail as well as outcome is part of learning to be more conscientious. Some people find this easy; many do not. But most tasks that work requires are skill-based and skills can be learned. Along with more constructive attitudes and outcomes.

Sharing common problems in a tolerant atmosphere, discussing openly the psychological pressures people may be feeling but not articulating, brainstorming new strategies as a team or staff group, providing and enthusiastically attending any and all professional development opportunities, naming skill deficits so that they can be addressed, and encouraging people to share their ideas are all straightforward ways to ensure higher levels of cooperation and make staff more confident and more efficient.

Even when a team change like this is not possible, we can learn to encourage ourselves to work smarter, with less fear and with greater enjoyment. Thinking about how we work, as well as work itself, shifts the terrain nicely. Feeling unafraid to make changes, and less fearful of making mistakes, you will find that work itself will inevitably be less stressful. It may even be surprisingly rewarding.

What Do You Owe Your Boss?

❧

Do you feel entitled to be paid because you are *at* your workplace, however little you are doing? Have you ever felt entitled to take off yet another Monday because, frankly, your weekend left you wrecked? What about resigning from your job by text message? Or reneging on a shift when there's no one else to take your place?

Have you ever left out crucial information in a report because it was too hard to collect? Or traded on colleagues' conscientiousness by doing much less than your share? And what about spilling the beans to a competitor? Or spending hours at work on Facebook or tweeting? Or looking for a better job on your current employer's time?

For many people, taking advantage of an employer is no more serious than a game, a way of asserting some independence perhaps, or rebelliousness. I am reminded as I write this how children of eight or nine sometimes say to an adult, "You're not the boss of me!"

Issues around loyalty, honesty and cooperation in the workplace aren't new. For all the talk of the good old days when at least some faithful souls joined a company or organization at fifteen and left forty or fifty years later with a hearty handshake and a handsome watch, there have always been fierce workplace tussles around loyalty and the exercise of power.

We know that employees are also vulnerable to exploitation. In fact, because of the inherent power biases, most of us are rather more aware of and sensitive to this than we are of employees letting bosses or managers down.

The examples of employee exploitation are indeed familiar. When companies restructure, the same demands may be left to far fewer people. People can be made redundant with no notice and minimum or no support. In many workplaces people are pushed to take on significant levels of extra responsibility for no additional rewards. It's also routine for low-paid employees to be required to attend meetings or training without receiving any pay for that time. Little extras that cost a company virtually nothing may be arbitrarily withdrawn. (One of our leading companies, posting profits in the billions, quite recently decided that tea and coffee should no longer be free: a startling example of corporate stupidity, given the cost in employee resentment.)

In other companies, training may be inadequate, undermining people's confidence to do their job well. People may be laid off by a company that can still afford lavish directors' bonuses. And of course anyone who works for a boss who is bad tempered, unpredictable, self-serving or plain incompetent will suffer, often seriously.

MOST OF US SPEND at least forty waking hours a week at our paid work, sometimes many more. Add on travel time, plus the time we spend thinking about work and extending our skills, or worrying about or recovering from our working day, and a vast chunk of our lives is accounted for.

We also take it for granted that people will routinely describe themselves in work terms: "I'm an accountant"; "I'm a dentist"; "I'm in retail." Our identity is always far, far greater than our career, but this is indicative of the degree to which our sense of self and our "work self" can merge.

What this means is that how we get along with our colleagues, how we are respected and appreciated by others at work, and especially how we feel about ourselves in our workplace role, inescapably affects our well-being and morale.

It also impacts on our physical health. But when it comes to these contentious issues of workplace expectations and entitlements it is the psychological impact that will be most powerful. The ethical issues are sensitive here, too, because when we do let a boss or organization down, we are invariably letting colleagues down too. And we are letting ourselves down when we are less conscientious than we could be (or so conscientious that we have no life other than work—that's at least as disastrous).

WORK, ALONG WITH intimacy and parenting, offers us our best chance to grow up. It pushes us to see that our agenda is just one among many. To benefit from that challenge we need to feel conscious that our choices are intrinsically empowering. However humble our role, we need to take on the inner challenge of working fairly and honestly, wherever we find ourselves.

From whichever side of the line you stand, this means applying the golden rule: *being* the colleague or boss you would most like to have. This might include not making self-serving excuses as to why you don't need to do your best. It might mean owning up to your choices and noticing how they are affecting other people. In some workplaces it might mean speaking up about complex issues that negatively affect other people. It might mean offering more support to those who are struggling. It will certainly mean noticing how your work, and particularly your attitudes toward work, are contributing to the person you are becoming.

Seeking Work

✺

Some work is exceptionally arduous. Australian writer Elisabeth Wynhausen (author of *Dirt Cheap*) and American writer Barbara Ehrenreich (*Nickel and Dimed*) have both written eloquently and persuasively about the particular stresses of low-paid, low-prestige work where sometimes quite complicated competencies are assumed without support, training or security.

As those two fine writers make clear, people accept terrible conditions when they have few choices. At any level of society, but particularly when people are living from one paycheck to the next, not having work is immensely stressful. And looking for work is often far more difficult and demeaning than it should be.

EMPLOYMENT STATISTICS are almost certainly fairly slippery. In my own circles alone I know of people who would not be counted among the unemployed but are certainly without adequate paid work. Or they have "retired" far earlier than they would have wished. I suspect, too, that significant numbers of people have no choice but to become consultants—with all too few opportunities to consult. And in all kinds of fluid areas from hospitality to building, writing and design, unknown numbers of freelancers and the self-employed must charge below breadline rates or do without the work on which they could once rely. (Large organizations also pay for freelance work ever later, treating it far too often as hobby income rather than as the butterless bread on which most freelancers subsist.)

JACK, a friend in his forties with three children, described to me his many months of spending hours each day trawling the Net for employment opportunities. "Soul destroying" was how he expressed it, especially when his many carefully structured applications went totally unacknowledged. More poignantly still, through this time he had somehow to maintain a stubborn belief in himself and his capabilities. As he put it, "With the mounting financial and family stress, I had to sustain a belief in myself or I couldn't look for jobs, never mind apply for them."

Until we are without secure work, Jack stressed, it is virtually impossible to see how much structure and affirmation we draw from it, as well as the income that's so necessary for everyday life and for that essential confidence that we can provide adequately for ourselves and those we love.

IN THE FACE of daily disappointments, it's a tough ask to expect people to keep up that stubborn self-belief my friend so accurately identified. Even those lucky enough to be naturally resilient, or to have a partner or family who can pick up the financial burdens, are going to be severely stretched. This makes it crucial to understand what might best support people in this situation or, indeed, in any situation where uncertainty and loss of confidence dominate.

The most basic list would include the need to discuss the situation with a helpful professional (in this instance, a recruitment specialist or business coach) to see how best you can reframe your work experiences, think more laterally about a wider range of possibilities, or retrain. When the cost of professional guidance seems prohibitive, it's worth asking a creative, business-minded friend to brainstorm with you.

On a more personal note, it helps to increase your contacts rather than withdrawing. A casual conversation can lead to new ideas, perhaps new contacts. It is also vital to throw off and resist any notions of shame. Becoming someone who is easy to help is challenging but it may be essential. (Many of us don't know how hard we are to help unless we think about it . . . checking our responses . . . the irritation or passivity that covers our fear.)

Keeping your whole self in focus, you need to exercise more than usual, ideally twice daily and leaving the house to do it. It's also essential to cut to a minimum any additional tension or stress in your life, not least rerunning on an endless loop any inner scenarios of injustice or fear. And, like anyone dealing with chronic stress, you need to eat healthily and well and cut down or cut out alcohol. In all but tiny amounts alcohol is a depressant that you can't emotionally or physically afford.

When the situation continues for many months, as it did for my friend Jack, the list might also include pushing to the top of your agenda any creative or social activity that lifts your spirits or connects you to the world beyond your own concerns. "Looking for work is a full-time job," Jack told me. But, as with any full-time job, there must be some balance and nourishment in other areas of your life.

. . .

THOSE CHANGES can make a difference, if only to your sense of personal power and choice. But what any person can do individually is, in my view, not nearly enough.

The loss or diminishment of paid work is a social problem, not just an individual one. Many people lose work for reasons that have nothing to do with them individually. And I know how hard people must fight to remind themselves that, as they search for work, the daily rejections they receive truly are not personal. In fact, this is doubly true. We may be turned down for reasons that have nothing to do with us and which we could never control or influence. (Perhaps someone was already in the job; perhaps the employer always wanted someone who is twenty-five when we are fifty, or fifty when we are twenty-five.) What's more, online applications make this grueling process even less personal. Many recruitment agencies and employers contact only the few people who make the short list. Far more often than not, the rest are left to guess at the outcome.

Because looking for work can be so tough—and so clearly lacking in ordinary warmth—I feel strongly that we need to resist this massive depersonalization. *We need to make finding work for those who want work a shared responsibility rather than a lonely and individual one.*

Wherever we are on the work continuum (in work, looking, retired), we could and we should make it our business to think harder and more creatively on behalf of those we know who are looking for work. We could make sure that our concern is practical as well as kind. We could make calls, network, think harder about long shots or less predictable connections, and offer genuine ideas rather than sympathy or indifference.

. . .

THE MOST CRUCIAL investment we can ever make is in our shared social well-being. So often it is personal contacts, a thoughtful introduction, or someone thinking freshly about how a person's experience might be used, that makes all the difference. I have been struck often by how relatively few people do step up and network in these ways. Yet the benefits for all could not be more significant.

Long Live the Weekend

✿

Our weekend is under threat. Our leisure times are under threat. And it matters.

Setting aside the prestige professions where the question of who "owns" our time is often murkiest, and also setting aside the perils of self-employment where seeking work can dominate to an alarming extent, currently most people working at nights and weekends are paid extra as recognition that they are *doing* extra. They are giving up time that they have every right to believe belongs to them rather than to their organization or employer. But as the weekend becomes an increasingly moveable feast, our confidence as a community that we have the right to claim time of our own becomes ever shakier.

This vexed question of how much time we "sell" in return for vital income is already significant. Speaking about work, many of us unthinkingly use "slave words" ("I can't . . ."; "I must . . ."; "We have to . . ."). Sometimes this is warranted, sometimes not, but it points to how powerless we can feel in the face of our career demands, especially when there are urgent practical issues involved like paying the mortgage and providing for our children.

. . .

SINCE THE INDUSTRIAL revolution brought vast numbers of people in from the fields and onto factory floors, and then increasingly into offices and service industries, social philosophers and commentators have warned against the dangers of people being seen and treated as economic units rather than as human beings with complex needs—only some of which are met by work.

When comparatively little time remains in the day, night or week that's *not* given over to paid work, or when we feel helpless about which hours we may be required to work, this goes straight to the heart of our sense of self.

Who are we, when we are not working? Do our lives have meaning, beyond our work role or paycheck? What kind of life is it anyway if we have no time for relationships, personal interests, reflection; no time for our creative passions; no time to care for our homes and communities?

However much we may like our work—and many people do indeed like their work, humble or not—we need a life outside it. If we live to work, or if we allow our sense of self to be defined by work, this may make us boring or depleted. It will certainly make us vulnerable. Losing our job, or reaching retirement age, can then appear catastrophic.

EVEN WHEN WORK is not our entire life, our psychological and physical well-being depends in great part on how healthy our personal relationships are. And that's where the precious weekend is needed.

"Keep holy the Sabbath" is a religious commandment that also makes powerful psychological and social sense. The point of the commandment is that we need specified and inviolate times when we turn our attention away from our external goals to remember who and what we care about, and what life is for.

In fact, to live fully we need time to care for our souls and spirits, perhaps our bodies too. We need time to deepen our essential relationships rather than giving them only our wrung-out, work-wearied self at the end of the day. Some of us need time for awe, wonder or God.

Most of us do indeed pride ourselves on our social relationships. We do believe that family, friends and community sustain us. We do believe some things are more important than making money. We are aware how seductive work can be and how necessary it is to keep our priorities straight.

Rebelling against the erosion of the weekend, and being clear about how much time we are "not for sale," affirms those values. It also develops us as more rounded, less vulnerable people. And it takes nothing from work when we are actually there.

No to Bullying

꙳

M ost people spend a staggering percentage of their waking
hours at work. This makes it not just worrying but totally
unacceptable if they have to put up with behavior from colleagues,
managers or bosses that fails to meet basic levels of consideration,
courtesy and respect.

It used to be that most bullies, sadists or misanthropes would,
like the rest of us, not only dress up for work but also curtail their
emotions and behavior there, saving their infantile rages, their self-
centered demands or their obscenities for those unfortunate enough
to live with them.

That seems to have changed—for the worse. Work is no longer
automatically a place where personal boundaries are routinely
respected. Or where courtesy can be taken for granted. Indeed,
asking the most tentative of questions I have been hearing some
hair-raising stories of bullying, shunning, undermining, manipula-
tion, sarcasm, unreasonable and contradictory demands, lying, disloyalty, unfair accusations, temper tantrums and sulking—often
delivered with a tremendous sense of entitlement and with virtually
no fear that these behaviors will harm the bully's career rather than
the people around them.

. . .

THERE IS SOMETHING seriously wrong here. Every company, every organization, whether in the private or public sector, has in place guidelines about how people should behave at work and be treated. It's just as clear what should happen when these guidelines are transgressed. Yet in none of the situations that I have been hearing about was there any expectation that this toxic behavior would be dealt with effectively. In fact, where the bullying culture goes all the way to the top, victims often feel powerless even to complain. That kind of silencing is itself a form of bullying and should never be tolerated in a contemporary workplace.

BECAUSE WE SEE others' behavior so subjectively, it can be difficult sometimes to prove bullying. After all, bullies are often highly adept at shifting their conduct depending on whether they are trying to impress someone or crush them. When bullying is covert, the victim needs to be listened to and protected. This will mean strictly avoiding being alone with the bully, keeping a record of the incidents, and talking about the situation publicly rather than taking on what should be the bully's shame.

Sometimes, though, the bully's behaviors are flagrant, with many people witnessing what they are doing, or feeling its effects. Yet still nothing is done. No one is cautioned or sacked. And often the bully's behavior will worsen as they recognize that there are, in fact, no external constraints.

Perhaps the most awful of these situations is when someone seems literally to gain power through their negativity: when bullying is mistaken for strength or when playing favorites or dividing and conquering is misunderstood as managing people.

IT SEEMS incredible that any twenty-first-century organization could ignore bullying, if only because it directly and inevitably affects their bottom line. Yet this, too, clearly happens.

It's so obvious that when people feel hurt, disregarded or frightened, they can't do their best work and often they can't do much work at all. It's also obvious that when bullying is tolerated, even those not directly affected will feel uneasy and betrayed. Morale will slump and so will the energy and effectiveness of the organization. But even these well-researched facts don't seem to be enough to shift some organizations out of their lethargy when it comes to bullying.

IT IS EASY to say that people should leave their job when bullying occurs. But even if this were always possible, and even if bullying were not so widespread, is that a solution? Insult is added to injury when it's the victim who is driven away, rather than the bully. What's more, it keeps alive the assumption that the victim must bear the pain *and* solve the situation.

We need to resist that kind of thinking. If bullying in the workplace is to stop, or at least cease to be tolerated and sometimes rewarded, we need a cultural change in how we think about it. This means regarding bullying in all its forms as unacceptable as any other form of violence. *It means naming it as a violence that can be deadly.* It means not giving in to the fantasy that these pathetic behaviors are strong—or inevitable.

. . .

THIS IS yet another situation where collective action is needed. The worse the culture of bullying, the more difficult it is for any lone individual to act effectively. This means that colleagues must get together to name what's going on and take a stand, ideally involving people outside their immediate organization wherever possible. Just as critical is for us, the wider public, to insist on zero tolerance when it comes to bullying. Bullying is often carried out in private. But, like any abuse, it is never a private matter.

Bullying can happen only when we shrug our shoulders or look away. Naming the problem as dangerous and unacceptable, *we need to hold the bullies unconditionally responsible for their behavior.* We need to avoid or ban suggestions that somehow victims bring it upon themselves, or deserve it. Or that bullies' psychological problems should excuse their behavior.

WHEREVER bullying is tolerated, it pollutes and eventually destroys any hope of a positive workplace culture. Its effects are widespread and can be long lasting. Keeping quiet, or looking the other way when bullying occurs, we do ourselves a tremendous injustice. Calling the bully on their obnoxious behaviors and refusing to tolerate them or collude with them, we save victims from further harm. We also save ourselves.

Workplace Listening

⚘

In every organization and workplace, listening skills matter. Whatever the business or service offered, communication is key and there can't be effective communication without listening. With the rise in awareness of emotional intelligence, listening skills—and communication skills more generally—are better appreciated than they once were. But that doesn't mean that they are widely enough practiced. One of the most common complaints against leaders and managers in business and government is that they don't know how to listen. Or they are not willing to listen. This frustrates the people around them. It also distances them.

To be a good listener takes a fair degree of humility as well as self-control and respect for others. Arrogance, indifference, self-absorption, shyness or a lack of curiosity or interest all get in the way of effective listening. So does a lack of confidence. Yet, if we were to think about it at all, most of us might assume that it is in our intimate relationships that listening matters most (or in the hour you spend with your therapist talking about how your partner never listens).

. . .

THIS ASSUMPTION is at least half true. Interested, open-minded listening can indeed revive and restore an intimate relationship. People can become real to one another in new and refreshing ways. It can become newly possible to *care*. But in workplaces, too, the value of listening with real interest cannot be underestimated. And given the time that we spend at work, and the dependence we have on healthy working relationships, "listening deficits" can loom extremely large.

People talking over one another; interruptions that make it impossible for people to express themselves coherently; emotive, racist or sexist language used to coerce or silence colleagues; trivializing or condemning people's opinions; silencing legitimate differences of opinion; "teasing" used to distance or hurt; an unwillingness to make the time that listening demands: all these difficulties and more affect countless people's working lives on a daily basis. What's more, they add considerably to the stress that many people already feel as they struggle with tough deadlines or conflicting demands, problems that themselves may be the result of poor communication and anxious or careless listening.

CAREFUL LISTENING takes more than a willingness to close our lips and open our ears. It demands that we step over our prejudices or expectations to hear what is actually being said. It certainly demands that we do actually *listen*, rather than composing our response or getting ready to bring the conversation back to ourselves. Time is sometimes given as a reason not to listen carefully, but it takes no more time to listen well than to listen badly. In fact, it may take less time when there are fewer hurts to heal or mis-understandings to unravel. It also makes life far more interesting when you are able to hear as well as listen.

Many people believe that listening is or ought to be natural. Yet how many of us truly know how to listen even to ourselves? Do we know how our tone of voice or manner of speaking sounds to other people? Or what attitudes and messages emerge along with our words? Are we aware of what we are conveying with our gestures, our body language, as well as our speech? Do we even notice when the conversation drones on relentlessly about our own concerns?

Listening to ourselves (at least sometimes), and *noticing* the effect we are having on others, is an essential first step in self-awareness. If we are cut off from hearing ourselves, or indifferent about how successfully we communicate and listen, then chances are that we may also have difficulty tuning in at any depth to other people.

WE LISTEN in order to hear something new. Or perhaps to share, to console, or pay our respects. Listening with care, we may even allow what we are hearing to change our perspective or opinions. We are also giving vital messages through how we listen, tuning some people in and tuning others out, offering—or withdrawing— interest, concern, respect.

Not listening to another person tells them that they don't matter (or their experiences or opinions don't matter). In workplaces, "not mattering" has real consequences. When colleagues, managers or bosses listen without interest, or fail to listen at all, the message is clear: "You don't matter. I don't need to understand you. You are essentially unimportant to me. And so are your ideas and experiences."

In some workplaces that painful message may be made through ignorance rather than intentionally. In one situation, described to me by a human resources manager in her thirties, middle managers were required to spend many hours (largely on their own time) analyzing and preparing complex proposals for change. They were then asked to present and brainstorm those ideas. When the decisions for change were made, however, their proposals were totally discounted. The process had provided the organization with a veneer of consultation. But no one with any real power had, in fact, been listening. As this manager explained, it wasn't so much that her directors were discounting the research but that it never occurred to them to reconsider their own ideas in the light of this new information.

CAREFUL LISTENING is so fundamental to effective communication that wherever organizational morale or productivity is low, it is highly likely that not listening or poor listening has become entrenched. It doesn't take costly consultants to change this. It takes a willingness to think about listening freshly: to see it not as a skill only but also as a core expression of mutuality and respect.

More attentive listening can be learned. This is far easier for some people than for others, but it's a heady thing for even the most impatient or reluctant listener to discover that they have more self-control and interest in others than perhaps they expected. It can become a relief to *listen*, rather than constantly pushing their own agenda.

In healthy organizations (as in healthy relationships), satisfying, respectful, *curious* communication will always get a high priority. Where thoughtful listening is valued and practiced, that's a trustworthy and stimulating place to be. And a rewarding one.

A Treasury of Kindness

W ork is where most of us rub shoulders with the greatest number of people. It's where our social skills and diplomacy are most needed. It's where our dependence on others is starkly demonstrated. It's where our ego and competitiveness may need the most taming. It's also where our decency will be sharpened as well as challenged.

There are countless opportunities in any working day to hone our capacities for kindness: to ease the difficult moments and celebrate the good ones. Whether we are face-to-face with clients or customers, or whether most of our contacts are with colleagues only, our most fundamental attitudes toward ourselves and other people will, in most workplaces, be constantly tested.

IN WORKPLACES where kindness, thoughtfulness and even courtesy are mistaken for weakness, the entire staff will feel undervalued and insecure. Far more common are situations where people simply feel too rushed to take the few seconds it needs to think and behave inclusively. Or just to notice when someone is struggling and to ask, "Can I help?"

A successful working life should and can include learning to support other people effectively, not just those who are "below" you in terms of power, but uniformly. This might mean actively encouraging others or listening with care even when you assume that you've heard it all before. It may include sharing information generously. Or taking your turn to do what is less pleasant or praised.

There are countless moments in every working day when a thoughtful word, timely help or simply interest will lift someone's spirits immeasurably. Those choices don't depend on seniority or status. Each of us can *be* the person who creates those moments. We can also be the person who is trustworthy, who doesn't gossip, who isn't petty, who gives other people the benefit of the doubt and is prepared to listen to and respect their explanations when things seem to have gone wrong. Each of those choices is empowering. It is strengthening to *be* the person who appreciates others: who looks for what is positive and is unafraid to comment on that.

Working closely with others brilliantly tests and extends the limits of our tolerance. Exceptional friendships can emerge in the workplace. Just as valuable is the capacity to get along with the people who may never be your friends but can be better understood, cooperated with—and perhaps increasingly liked.

We can't choose our relatives, the old saying goes. Nor can we choose our workmates or colleagues. What we can do is choose the qualities that we are willing to value and express in the workplace *regardless of how humble or exalted our position is.*

COMPETITIVENESS is rife in many workplaces, not only around issues of job security, pay and promotion, but also reflecting the keen desire to be appreciated and noticed. "Am I doing this right?" is frequently code for "Am *I* all right?"

In that atmosphere, it is all too easy to attribute your own fears or inner criticisms to other people, to assume that they are thinking about you harshly or critically when this may not be the case at all. Or to interpret fairly mild remarks or comments as though they were negative. The best "cure" here is to be a careful observer of your patterns of interpretation. Are they generally encouraging? Are you clinging to habits of insecurity that you could now let go? Are you prepared to give others—and yourself—the benefit of the doubt? Are you able to get a lift from whatever words of appreciation come your way, rather than dwelling only on actual or perceived hurts or rebuffs? Are you willing to risk *putting other people at ease*?

IN ANY SITUATION we do best when we can claim our emotional power. Power is a complex issue in any workplace: who has it; who doesn't. Claiming your power to bring your highest values to your workplace—and live them out—will vastly benefit your sense of identity and inner security. It will also shift your perspective on how you value your time, your life and yourself.

Peacemaker's Power

Making peace, creating peace, desiring and *being* peace isn't work. It's all of life. But work is one of the places where we can rise to this challenge and meet it. And it is certainly where I wanted to complete this book on kindness.

It is impossible to think about kindness without considering harmony between people, and the happiness as well as safety and trust that brings. And it's impossible to think about harmony without thinking of the daily choices that add up to authentic, sustaining peacemaking.

Over the years I have written a number of versions of this short commitment. I have used them in my writings and in my teaching. I have sent them out via my website's Universal Heart Network and, more recently, via my Facebook page.

Many of you have responded positively, letting me know that you have been using this commitment, printing it out, sharing it with others; how you have secured it to your fridge next to a picture of the baby, or on a bulletin board at school or work. Or how you have tucked it into your daily journal or wallet to unfold when you need it.

That engagement with these words, and their powerful intention, means everything to me. Choosing which version to use here I returned to the first and simplest:

As a peacemaker I will . . .
Develop peace within my own heart and mind.
See the good in myself and other people.
Give others the benefit of the doubt.
Regard life as a precious gift.
Take time to look deeply and to listen.
Practice kindness—regardless of who "deserves" it.
Take responsibility for how I affect others.
Protect the vulnerable.
Learn from my mistakes.
Speak to myself like a true friend.
Notice what I already have.
Soften my reactiveness.
Accept difference—even when it challenges me.
Extend my vision of community to embrace all living beings.
Honor the earth and protect it, and all its living forms.
Learn the value of silence and of thoughtful speech.
Practice the power of forgiveness.
Open the space for joy, spirit and illumination to come in.
Cultivate gratitude for all that I am and all that you are.
Refuse violence as a solution to human problems—ever.
See the unity in all of life.
Live as a source of peace and kindness for others. And also for
     myself.

ABOUT THE AUTHOR

Stephanie Dowrick, Ph.D., has been writing on some of the most significant issues in contemporary life for many years. Her best-selling books include *Intimacy and Solitude, Forgiveness and Other Acts of Love, Choosing Happiness, Creative Journal Writing, In the Company of Rilke* and *Seeking the Sacred.* Described by the writer SARK as a "genius of the inner worlds," Dr. Dowrick has also written successful fiction and, before she took up writing as her main work, founded and was the first managing director of the London independent publishers the Women's Press. A trained psychotherapist, she has had a small private practice for many years, but now works mainly with groups in a wide variety of psychological and spiritual settings. Dr. Dowrick was ordained in 2005 by the New Seminary, New York, and is an adjunct fellow in the Writing and Society Research Group, University of Western Sydney, where she also completed her doctoral studies. The mother of two adult children, she has made her home in Sydney, Australia, since 1983.

Visit www.stephaniedowrick.com

Or meet her on the Official Stephanie Dowrick Facebook page.

www.facebook.com/StephanieDowrick

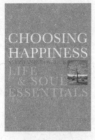

In *Choosing Happiness* the focus is on the only place where real change can happen: in how you see yourself and relate to other people. Ultimately, the message of this book is very simple: Right now, you can be happier!

In this exceptionally positive and encouraging book, Stephanie Dowrick sets free the journal writer that—she believes—is in virtually everyone. Through stories, examples and exercises, Dowrick shows that a genuine sense of possibility can be revived on every page.

Through her intimate, beautiful and encouraging writing, Dowrick shows that it is only in altering our perception— seeing all of life as sacred—that we will challenge the usual stories about who we are and what we are capable of being. *Seeking the Sacred* is a provocative and accessible read for those contemplating God, faith, spirituality and the nature of belief in twenty-first-century life.

In the Company of Rilke is a rare book about a rare poet. Rainer Maria Rilke was a giant of twentieth-century writing who remains a visionary voice for our own time, captivating readers not only with his brilliance but also his fearlessness about the "deepest things." Drawing on her deep understanding of the gifts of Rilke's writings, as well as her own personal spiritual seeking, Stephanie Dowrick offers an intimate and accessible appreciation of this most exceptional poet and his transcendent work.